NO WITNESSES

NO WITNESSES

An MJ Lange Murder Mystery

CINDY KLUDT

Copyright © 2023 by Cindy Kludt

No Witnesses

An MJ Lange Murder Mystery

All rights reserved. No part of this publication may be reproduced, distributed or transmitted in any form or by any means, including photocopying, recording, or other electronic or mechanical methods, without the prior written permission of the publisher, except in the case of brief quotations embodied in critical reviews and certain other noncommercial uses permitted by copyright law.

Although the author and publisher have made every effort to ensure that the information in this book was correct at press time, the author and publisher do not assume and hereby disclaim any liability to any party for any loss, damage, or disruption caused by errors or omissions, whether such errors or omissions result from negligence, accident, or any other cause.

Adherence to all applicable laws and regulations, including international, federal, state and local governing professional licensing, business practices, advertising, and all other aspects of doing business in the US, Canada or any other jurisdiction is the sole responsibility of the reader and consumer.

Neither the author nor the publisher assumes any responsibility or liability whatsoever on behalf of the consumer or reader of this material. Any perceived slight of any individual or organization is purely unintentional.

The resources in this book are provided for informational purposes only and should not be used to replace the specialized training and professional judgment of a health care or mental health care professional.

Neither the author nor the publisher can be held responsible for the use of the information provided within this book. Please always consult a trained professional before making any decision regarding treatment of yourself or others.

For more information, email kludt@mac.com

ISBN: 979-8-89109-713-1 (Paperback)
ISBN: 979-8-89109-714-8 (Ebook)

Get Your Free Gift!

Attention all crime drama and psychological thriller fans!

I am excited to share with you a glimpse into the backstory of wounded healer, psychologist, MJ Lange.

What happened to her as a teenager that led to her struggles with alcoholism and fueled her desire to save and help people, even if it meant putting herself in perilous situations while solving the mysteries?

If you love to understand the inner psychological working of the mind, this prequel will satisfy that need.

You can read the prequel of the MJ Lange mystery series by visiting:

https://cindykludtauthor.com/free-prequel

With love to Molly

Chapter 1

"Hi, I'm MJ and I'm an alcoholic."

It was my third meeting that week where I accepted a three-month chip. Three months sober. It had taken me nine months to get three consecutive months living without taking a drink of alcohol.

Of course, I had my reasons for why I needed to drink. Anyone would stay drunk if a client of theirs had put a gun to his mouth and blew his head off in front of them.

But the irony here is that quite possibly I wasn't able to stop this from happening because I had been drunk right before he did it. And then I had to drink to stop the endless and never-ending guilt I felt for his death.

My AA sponsor, Big Al, had come up to me and given me his bear hug, practically lifting me off the floor as he squeezed me. I don't think he had any idea how strong he was and I felt myself gasping for breath until he released me.

I looked up into his grinning face and somberly said, "Thanks Al, I couldn't have done this without you."

I realized that three months was nothing, but it was a big deal to me. I felt good, better than I've felt since my husband Gideon died on the operating table over two years ago when undergoing a liver transplant. That's when the heavy drinking began. I was overcome with remorse and guilt because I had persuaded him to get the transplant when he was against it. He had done it for me. And he died. I know he would have eventually succumbed to his cancer, but in my mind he could have had several years before that happened, and I hadn't given him that chance by insisting he get the transplant—all for selfish reasons.

My drinking after his death led me to act out in a couple of other entanglements which led to more guilt and more drinking. I felt I had no other choice but to drown myself in alcohol. It was either that, or death. I chose to live, but didn't realize until recently that the alcohol was just a slower way to die. Now I really had to choose life.

I finally had three months sober, was starting to feel alive again, and in many ways I was starting to forgive myself. Maybe there was something positive to say about the AA program. I wish my father had given it a chance instead of taking the chicken way out and ending his own life when I was only a teenager.

My best friend, Franny, was waiting to take me out for brunch after my AA meeting. She was very proud of me and my best cheerleader in me getting sober.

As I left the church where my meeting had taken place, I felt my cellphone buzz. When I looked to see who was calling, I stopped short, contemplating if I should answer or not.

I heard Franny calling out to me to get my attention. She was parked across the street so I put my phone back in my purse and hurried across to climb into the passenger side of her car.

"How did it go in there?"

I looked at my friend and smiled. She had no idea what AA was all about, or how difficult it had been for me to keep my sobriety going these past nine months.

"It was fine, Franny. Just fine. I took a three-month chip. No big deal."

But that was a lie. It *was* a big deal to me. I just didn't want to have to explain it all to Franny. Our relationship has had its ups and downs. It had become a bit strained as I was trying to maintain my sobriety.

I hadn't felt as close to her in the past nine months. Franny needed to be the one in charge and needed to come first. I had always played second fiddle to her. But during my attempt at recovery, I was told that I needed to put myself first, a difficult thing for me to do. I was a psychologist and by nature I wanted to help people and often didn't take proper care of myself and my own needs.

"Jesse just called me."

"No way, what did he want?"

"I didn't answer."

"Did he leave a message?"

"I haven't looked."

"Well, dang, MJ, look already, will you?"

"I'm not sure I need any kind of complications right now. I'm just learning how to be sober and to trust myself. I don't want to get entangled with any kind of relationship right now.

I got my heart broken once already, being vulnerable with him. I don't think I can handle anything like that again."

Franny remained silent and didn't press me on this issue. I knew she was trying hard to understand what I was going through and I appreciated it.

"Let's just go have a nice brunch, okay? I'll call him back later to see what he wants."

But the unanswered call left its mark. I tried to ignore it as we ate our food. I did wonder why Jesse was calling me after all this time. We had gotten close after he took three bullets when caught in the crosshairs between the drug dealer, Mike Rimichi, and my anonymous caller, Joe, who was murdered by Rimichi.

Jesse and I were on our way to some kind of relationship, when his estranged wife asked him to try again—for the children. I hadn't talked to him these past nine months. Now, all I wanted to do was finish eating and call him; so pathetic.

Of course I knew better than to do that without checking in with Big Al. My three-months sobriety was fragile and I knew that anything of an emotional nature could send me right back to drinking again.

During my struggle with sobriety, I was consumed with loneliness. I yearned for a partner. I knew that connecting back with Jesse would not be good for me.

Aunt Carrie, my neighbor, had her daughter April and her four-year-old granddaughter Joey, move in with her when Joey's father proved to be an abuser. Watching the interaction between April and her daughter made the grief of not having my own child with Gideon, my deceased husband, even stronger. I had always wanted children and it was in our plan to have several. But when Gideon was diagnosed with liver cancer, all of our plans for having children ceased.

Playing and engaging with Joey this past year lifted my heart and I slowly came to fall in love with her. Just listening to her little voice count, "one, two, three. . ." as I hid in an easy place for her to find me, caused me to giggle like a child myself when we'd play-hide-and-go-seek. I can't imagine feeling more love than what I feel for her, except maybe if I had my own child.

Chapter 2

After brunch with Franny, she dropped me off at my car near the church where the AA meeting had been held. There was a tangible tension I had felt between us at brunch. I felt a deep sadness around our struggling friendship. I was told that this kind of thing might happen when I no longer used alcohol to numb myself. Things that never bothered me before started to bother me about Franny. I was having a difficult time coping with the confusion it brought.

When I got home, I saw Aunt Carrie's car, so I crossed over to the gate that separated our two homes and walked up the steps to knock on her back door. I didn't want to be alone and she was like a balm to my nerves. Her door was always open to me.

I heard her call out to come in. I opened the door, which she never locked, and stepped into her kitchen. I immediately knew something was off. Her kitchen was usually warm and inviting with smells of cinnamon and delicious spices, indicating that Aunt Carrie had just taken some scrumptious dessert out of the oven, or she had some delicious food cooking on the stove.

Instead, as I walked further into the kitchen, I felt a chill. Instead of bright sunlight and delicious smells, it seemed dark and a bit dank.

"Aunt Carrie?"

"I'm in the living room."

As I walked into the living room, I saw her sitting in her rocking chair, rocking herself slowly and deliberately, her back straight and her eyes staring out. I could tell she had been crying.

"What's wrong?" I said with alarm.

Aunt Carrie was like the mother I never had. I loved our connection and counted on her for support. The sight of tears streaking down her face made me rush to her side and squat before her.

Her hands felt cold and limp as I took them in mine, "Aunt Carrie, what's happened?"

She stopped rocking, but she didn't look at me and continued to stare out at nothing.

I sat with her for a couple of minutes before I asked, "Did someone die?"

Then a terrible thought occurred to me and I asked her if it was her daughter, April, or worse, Joey. They were her life and I knew that if something happened to one of them she wouldn't be able to cope. As strong as she always appeared, I knew that any harm to one of them would take her down. And I had to admit that I was becoming close friends with April in addition to my loving connection to Joey.

Aunt Carrie wasn't my biological aunt. Everyone called her Aunt Carrie. She was a sixty-eight year old midwestern transplant to Los Angeles. She moved from the Midwest to be with her daughter and granddaughter four years ago and still acted as if she was living in a small town. She often left her back door unlocked and welcomed anyone into her home. She never failed to have some kind of dessert and a pot of coffee to offer her guests. I loved her for her stability and wholesomeness. She had taken me under her wing as a protective mother hen years ago.

At the mention of April and Joey, she finally blinked and looked at me. "She lost. Alex gets Joey fifty percent of the time."

I let out the breath I had been holding in, "I'm so sorry, Aunt Carrie. How is April taking it?"

"Better than me, I guess. She's upset, of course, but there isn't anything to be done about it right now. That bastard will use this win as a way to manipulate and continue to control April. You know it, and I know it. My heart breaks for both of them."

April's partner, Alex, had been emotionally and psychologically abusive since before Joey was born. But April finally found the courage to leave him.

I had been living with Aunt Carrie while my burned house was being rebuilt when April finally found the courage to leave Alex. At that time she and Joey moved in with Aunt Carrie and I moved into my small, remodeled therapy office over my garage.

The problem for April was that she never reported any abuse because Alex hadn't been physically abusive. She lacked evidence to prove her case that he would be an unfit parent for

Joey. Thus, she was thrown into a custody battle for Joey and had requested monitored visits for Alex.

April and Joey had moved into their own apartment after staying with Aunt Carrie for about six months. Her lawyer thought if she had her own place and could prove she could manage the finances and child care, alone, that would be in her favor when the custody hearing happened. But I guess not. April lost and had to give her precious child over to a man who hadn't paid any attention to his daughter until April left him. Only then did he try to get full custody.

As a psychologist I understood the mentality of an abuser. They often used custody battles as a way of controlling or getting even with their partners.

I hated that this was happening to them. Since I had grown to love little curly, blond-haired Joey, I felt bereft when her mother moved them out of Aunt Carrie's house. They still visited, but it wasn't the same as seeing them almost daily. I had started to see April and Joey as a part of my extended family and wished they still lived next door.

"What does this mean, Aunt Carrie? Is it over, or is there still something April and her lawyer can do to get full custody?"

She let out a deep sigh and tears gathered in her eyes, "I don't know, MJ. I don't know."

"Why don't you come over to my place for a while, Aunt Carrie? I'll make you a cup of coffee and I'm pretty sure I have some cookies in the cupboard."

She laughed at this because I was the worst cook and we both knew it. I was trying to do for her what she always did for me: ply me with coffee and sugar.

I laughed along with her as she started to stand. I helped her up and she headed to the kitchen where she started bustling around making her bitter coffee. She then opened her freezer and produced a package of what looked like her homemade frozen chocolate chip cookies—my favorite.

"Aunt Carrie, I should be taking care of you, not you fixing something for me."

"MJ, making coffee for you and eating these cookies with you, *is* you taking care of me. You lighten my day. You always do. Now sit down and tell me what you've been up to."

I wasn't surprised at her ability to put her own distress away, as she encouraged me to talk about myself.

I reminded her about my three-month sobriety chip, and then we discussed whether or not I should call Jesse back as we drank her bitter coffee and ate her warmed up chocolate chip cookies.

When I left, we both felt better. I thanked the stars for her living next door to me. She was like a warm blanket for me and I hoped that I had a similar effect on her. I hoped that April and Joey felt the same way about me as I did about them; that we were family.

As I walked back to my place over the garage, I looked at my almost finished newly rebuilt house. But instead of excitement, I couldn't shake a strong disturbing feeling that ran through my body about what Aunt Carrie just told me about April. I didn't feel good about it. I hoped that April didn't get sucked into going back to live with her abuser in order to protect her daughter from him, like many mothers do.

I had to remind myself that it was out of my control. They hadn't asked for my help and I didn't have any authority anyway. But as a friend to April, I decided that I would support her as best I could.

My phone buzzed as I entered my apartment and when I saw who it was, I was able to shake off the bad feeling I had about April.

Chapter 3

It was Jesse. He was calling again. I hadn't yet talked to Big Al about being in touch with Jesse again so I let the call go to my voicemail. If I only knew what it was he wanted then I'd be able to make the right decision, or at least get Big Al's opinion about it.

I waited a bit to see if he left a detailed message, busying myself with this and that in my little apartment.

When I saw he had left a message, I sat on my therapy chair and listened.

"Hey, MJ."

This was followed by a pause before he started in again, "I know this may seem out of the blue to you and I wouldn't be surprised if you ignored my calls after what happened."

There was another pause; this one longer, "I guess this was a bad idea. Calling you, I mean."

That was the end of the message.

What the hell?

I could feel myself getting angry that he didn't tell me what he was calling about so I could decide if I wanted to call him back or not. I was left with uncertainty and started to feel confused as the old yearning desire for him resurfaced.

I immediately wanted a drink. Damn him for causing this disruption in my quest for peace. Needing a drink was definitely a reason not to call him back.

After nine months of waffling between drinking and sobriety, I learned to pick up the phone and call my sponsor. But before I called Big Al, the crazy justifications started pretty quickly. I decided that I should find out what Jesse wanted so I had something tangible to tell Big Al. This is how I justified calling him back, my hands shaking as I punched in his number.

It was a big mistake.

The minute he answered I felt myself being pulled toward him. His voice was warm and friendly and I imagined his muscular arms bulging under his t-shirt as his bicep tattoos peaked out. There was always a sense of him being a 'bad boy,' ignoring the rules, but always for justice. I envisioned him working for the helpless and the victims of crimes, even if he had to break a few rules, which is what in fact he had done in the past.

"What do you want, Jesse?" I tried to harden my voice, but wasn't very successful at it.

"MJ, it's good to hear your voice. I've missed you."

So this was how he was going to play it? He missed me? After deciding to go back to his wife? The wife who was filing for divorce and had been living with another man?

"What do you want, Jesse?"

I took a deep breath and was determined not to talk until he explained himself. I needed to find out why he was calling me. It was dangerous for my sobriety to be talking to him, so I waited for him to give me a straight answer.

"MJ."

I let the silence deepen, but I have to admit, I practically had to bite my tongue to keep from expressing all the pent up emotion I had been repressing since I got his first call.

"MJ," he tried again.

I couldn't help myself so I said, "Saying my name over and over again doesn't really help. Jesse, why did you call me? Just say it."

"Okay. I heard about what happened with your client. I tried to reach out to you back when it happened but you never returned my calls or texts. I figured you didn't want to talk to me."

"Okay. You got the message back then. I assume that nothing's changed in your life, so why are you calling me?"

"Because I can't stop thinking about you. I can't stop worrying about you. I don't know how you're doing and it's driving me crazy."

"Jesse, this right here is inappropriate. You're a married man. You shouldn't be having these feeling about me, or if you have them, you need to figure out how you're going to deal with them; but not with me."

"I know. I know. It was a bad idea to call you, but I needed to hear your voice. I needed to know you were okay. Jeez, MJ, you were working your way out of a horrid, near fatal death and then I hear that your client blew himself away in front of you. I know you, MJ. You would have taken that to heart. You would have been feeling responsible and guilty. I know that about you."

He did know me. He was intimately involved with the incident where I was almost murdered. He was also the only one, besides Franny, who knew about what happened with my father's suicide. He knew how riddled with guilt I was over that; still am.

The truth was that hearing his voice and his concern had me going. I wanted to share everything with him. I wanted to share all my fears, my struggles with alcohol, and most of all my need for someone to hold me and make me feel safe.

"Jesse, I won't lie. I am struggling with feelings of guilt. I'm struggling with my use of alcohol to numb myself. I'm struggling to feel confident again. I feel like tragedy seems to follow me. Count yourself lucky that you got away from me so quickly. You're better off without me."

"No, MJ, I want to be there for you; to protect you. Can we at least be friends? Can you let me worry about you and use any kind of influence I may have to help you feel protected and secure?"

Oh my, I wanted so badly to say yes, to tell him I needed him. I wanted his protection. I wanted all he could give me. I wanted to take any little tiny thing I could get. But I knew this was dangerous territory for me and for him. I knew without even having to call Big Al, that this could be my downfall. One meeting with Jesse, or even another phone call with him, could get me confused and drinking again. Having anything to do with a married man was just wrong. But that didn't mean that I didn't have feelings for him.

I took a deep breath and regretfully said, "I know you mean well, Jesse, but any kind of contact with you is dangerous for me. Just know that I'm doing the things that are good for me and I have the support that I need right now. Please respect what I'm saying and don't call me again."

With that I disconnected from him and then I called Big Al. I knew that if I didn't call my sponsor, or go to a meeting, the call would trigger so many emotions and thoughts that would drive me straight to my favorite shot of vodka.

I counted this as a win for me. I knew that Jesse was probably unhappy with his wife and probably regretted going back to her. Since he did it for his kids, he most likely felt that he couldn't just up and leave. And I agreed. It wouldn't be fair to the kids. He shouldn't have gone back to her in the first place. I'm guessing he was struggling with his decision and reached out to me thinking that maybe I would have an answer for him.

I didn't, and felt sad that we never got the chance to see where our connection could have gone. I imagine he was feeling the same way.

Chapter 4

The next day, I gave April a call to commiserate with her. We had become close friends during her time as my next door neighbor and I wanted her to know that I was there to support her.

Plus, I loved Joey and had often babysat her to give both April and Aunt Carrie a break. Joey was a lot to handle. She was a bundle of energy and trying to keep up with her took its toll, but I enjoyed every minute of it—most of the time.

When April answered the phone, I could hear the strain in her voice. "Hi April. I heard. I'm so sorry."

I let her cry for a while before I asked if she'd like me to come over or if she'd like to come over to my place. She told me that she was just about to head over to her mother's place, so I told her I'd meet her there.

I was shocked when I saw April. She had lost weight and her clothes fit loosely on her slim frame. Her eyes were red from crying and the dark circles made her look haunted.

Joey clung to her mother and looked upset. But when she saw me, she broke into a smile and ran over to give me a hug. I picked her up and swung her around, which was our usual greeting. Then I walked over to April and gave her a hug.

April and Joey sat at the kitchen table as Aunt Carrie bustled around the kitchen making lunch for us all. I pulled a chair out to join them, after Aunt Carrie refused my help. Joey came and sat on my lap, asking me if I had a surprise for her.

I gave her a squeeze and said in a high falsetto, "No, I don't have a surprise for you today," and then released her and looked at April with concern.

"You didn't go to work today, April?" I asked.

"I took the day off. I just couldn't make myself do anything. I couldn't even make Joey breakfast."

I could see she was depressed. There was no light in her eyes and her shoulders were slumped. I remember saying to myself, *This isn't good.*

When lunch was ready, we all sat around the kitchen table eating. I could see that April only picked at her food.

"April, you have to eat," Aunt Carrie said.

"I know, Mom. I'm just not hungry. I can't believe I was so stupid."

"You can't beat yourself up about this, Honey. It was out of your control."

"I should have left the minute I found out I was pregnant. I should have never let him even know I was pregnant."

I could hear the self-recrimination in her voice and my heart ached for her. "April, you didn't do anything wrong. He did; not you."

We were all avoiding saying Alex's name since Joey was sitting at the table listening to everything we were saying. She remained very quiet, as if she knew we were discussing something important that pertained to her. But I have to say that I honestly didn't care anymore if she heard how bad her dad was. We weren't saying anything that little girl didn't already know. She hated it when she had to go with him. It tore at April's heart every time she had to let her go.

It was a solemn lunch. No one had much more to say. Even Joey was quiet and actually started to suck her thumb, something I hadn't seen for a long time. As a therapist, I could see that she was regressing with all the stress and I wanted to fix it for her so badly. If she were my child, I knew it would kill me to be in April's situation.

After we finished eating, Aunt Carrie suggested that April and I go for a walk together and she'd look after Joey.

Joey did not want to us go, but was bribed with the promise of ice cream with her grandmother.

April and I walked to the beach and sat watching the waves come and go. I didn't say anything, but just sat with her as she allowed the rhythmic crashing of the waves to soothe her.

When she finally spoke, a chill went through my body. "You know, MJ, I had a feeling that the court would do what they did. Now I won't be able to protect my little girl."

I did not know how to respond, so I remained silent, knowing that if I told her that it would all work out, it would only be hollow words.

The next weeks went by quickly as I focused on my sobriety and my work. However, I wasn't happy about Aunt Carrie's worries about April and Joey. I tried to distract her and spend more time with her at her house, even persuading her to go back to her beloved bridge card games. I have to admit that I was also worried, but didn't know what to do.

I called April every day. I was concerned about her statement about not being able to protect Joey. I didn't know if Alex was capable of hurting his daughter or not. When I asked her if she felt Alex would harm Joey, she denied that he would. She told me that she was more concerned about how it would affect Joey in the long run, and I felt the same way.

Big Al had been attempting to teach me to focus on me and not on everyone else. He was right. I was so conditioned to look after everyone else, that it just seemed like normal behavior to me. But this was a small child we were talking about. She didn't have a choice in the matter. It was up to us as adults to protect her and how would we do that if the legal system allowed this?

Aunt Carrie was special to me and I felt compelled to do something to help her feel better. She had stopped going to her bridge games all together when April and Joey had moved in with her. But they hadn't been living with her for months and she still hadn't gotten back to her social events. I knew she was depressed and worried about what would happen between April and Alex. However, her biggest concern was what would happen to little Joey being caught in the middle of their custody battle.

I was worried too. I'd seen enough in my private practice to know how bad things could turn out when a woman leaves an abusive situation. My concern for April was that Alex was getting back at her by trying to get more custody of Joey. He knew that would hurt her the most.

My blood boiled at just the thought of sweet little Joey having to be anywhere near that man.

The courts had decided and now it was up to April to see if she and her lawyer could change their mind. What probably had to happen was for Alex to do something illegal, or to openly harm April or Joey in some way before the 50/50 custody would be changed.

I knew that Alex was too smart to do anything that stupid. He wasn't a physical abuser, but a psychological and emotional one. He was very crafty about how he manipulated. He could charm the pants off of anyone, so it was difficult to prove how toxic he was.

The thing that riled me the most was that he had absolutely no interest in little Joey until April left him. All of a sudden he then wanted custody? I felt so hopeless and powerless about the situation. And if I felt that strong about it, April and Aunt Carrie must have been going absolutely nuts.

Since worrying about others and trying to control their lives is a co-dependent trait and very common in adults who had been raised by an alcoholic, Big Al suggested that I go to Al-anon meetings in addition to AA meetings. He felt I was a perfect candidate for it. He observed that my whole life was about making sure everyone else was happy. If I could fix anything for someone else, I'd do it, even at a cost to myself.

So far, I hadn't and still have not gone to an Al-anon meeting. I know that my resistance to going is strong. I justify it by telling myself that my AA meetings keep me busy enough.

It had been several weeks since Jesse called and I felt like I was making progress in letting him go. I tried to focus on what it was I needed to do for myself. I made outgoing calls to newer members of AA. I did everything Big Al told me to do. I finally felt that maybe I was letting go of my grand need for control.

I heard over and over again at my meetings that just when you think you've licked a bad habit, something happens to prove you wrong. All the shit comes raining down again and it's like you've never made any progress in the first place.

And that is exactly what happened.

It was early on a Wednesday morning in July. The sun was already beating down hot. I had finally bought shades for my windows in my office apartment and had them drawn to keep the heat out. I hadn't gotten central air for my office because most of the time when one lived near Venice Beach, one didn't need it because there was usually a nice breeze from the ocean and I could just open my windows and let the cool air in.

I remember feeling that I wished I had air conditioning because it was already hot in my place; even with the two fans I had positioned around the joint.

My phone buzzed and I looked to see who was calling so early.

It was Aunt Carrie, which was unusual because she would usually text me to come join her for her famous sweet rolls. She worried that she might wake me if she called, even though I had told her that I was an early riser.

"Hello, Aunt Carrie, what's up?"

I could tell she had been crying as she cried into the phone, "MJ, you have to come over. Something terrible has happened. APRIL'S DEAD."

I just stood there, my hand on my coffee cup, about to take my first sip of the morning. I wasn't comprehending. "Aunt Carrie, what?"

I heard her sobbing and immediately said, "I'm on my way."

Oh my god, oh my god. April's dead? What the hell happened?

I flew out of my apartment and took the steps down two at a time, barefoot and by a miracle did not step on a nail or other construction debris as I hurried over to her house to be with her.

When I got to her back door, I didn't knock; I hurried into the house as I called out to her. It was the first time I didn't think about admonishing her for leaving her back door unlocked.

I followed the sounds of her sobs into the living room and saw her sitting on her sofa with an officious looking man and woman sitting across from her.

The woman stood and introduced herself as Detective Myer, then turned and introduced her partner, Detective Dunham. Detective Myer stated that she was grateful that I was able to come and be with Aunt Carrie.

"What happened?" I sat down next to Aunt Carrie and gently put my arm around her shoulders. I could feel her shudder as she let out a long mournful breath.

My first thought was that Alex had murdered April. I sat beside Aunt Carrie and held my breath. All I could think about was poor little Joey losing her mommy.

Detective Myer seemed to be the one more in charge, or maybe she was just the one who was more sympathetic to Aunt Carrie's plight.

She explained that in the early morning hours, there was a 911 call from April's house from a little girl who told the operator that her mommy wasn't in the house. When asked how old she was, Joey had told them that she was four years old.

Apparently the operator had Joey stay on the phone while they were able to determine her exact location and send out a team to investigate. Joey had been able to stay on the phone until someone came to the door. She had been taught how to open her mother's cellphone and to punch the emergency button if she were ever alone or scared. She was also taught not to ever let anyone into the house without her mother being there. When the policemen came, she steadfastly kept the door locked and they had to break it down to get to her.

What a brave little girl.

My heart ached for her and for Aunt Carrie, who let out a long wail at this point in Detective Myer's narrative. I got goosebumps throughout my body as I braced myself for what I was about to hear.

Detective Myer explained that April was found outside leaning against the back door. She didn't have a pulse. The policemen who answered the emergency call determined that she was dead and the detectives were called in for a suspicious death. Gratefully, she did not go into any gory details, but our imaginations were probably worse than the reality.

"What happened? She was so young. What was she doing outside? How did she die?" I jumped in with so many questions.

"Detective Dunham and I were called to the location, along with the medical examiner. The ME's initial discovery is that it appears to be death by strangulation, but we have to wait for the autopsy to make that official."

At this, Aunt Carrie could no longer contain herself as she jumped up and started pacing randomly around the room, chanting, "No, no, no, no, no. It can't be. He did it. He finally did it. Now he gets everything he wants."

She was inconsolable, so I let her pace until a thought came to my mind and said, "Detective Myer, where's the little girl? Where's Joey?"

Chapter 5

Immediately after I asked the question, Aunt Carrie pulled herself together and stared at the detectives. She didn't have to say anything. I knew what she was thinking.

"Is she with her father?" I asked.

It had to be asked. Both Aunt Carrie and I were thinking the same thing: if it was Alex who strangled April, then Joey might also be in danger if she was with her father.

"The little girl was taken in by social services who will be handling her care. We haven't yet been able to contact her father."

"Oh my god! They're going to give her to Alex? He's a very bad man. That can't happen." Aunt Carrie was near hysterics.

"Aunt Carrie, we don't know that yet. Let's let these detectives explain what's to be done."

I turned to them and said, "Will her father be the one to take her? Even if he's under suspicion?"

Detective Myer looked at her partner and I saw the look they gave each other. I interpreted that look to say that until they had a warrant for Alex's arrest, their hands were tied.

I wanted to scream and stamp my feet in frustration. The thought that Alex, who probably killed April, would be able to take charge of our sweet little Joey who had just lost her mother was unthinkable.

Aunt Carrie was beside herself and I knew that I couldn't afford to lose my cool. I needed to be strong for her. The nightmare she was experiencing just got worse.

"Aunt Carrie," I said, "let's not get ahead of ourselves here. We are both in shock right now. I'm sure there will be an autopsy and a full investigation. If they suspect Alex, which most likely they will, you can petition Child Protective Services as the next of kin and bring her home with you."

I turned to Detective Myer and said, "Isn't that right, Detective Myer?"

"Child Protective Services has the child right now until her father can be located. If we can't find him, they will most likely reach out to you. They will want to determine if the child saw anything that would be traumatic to her. If she did see something, then she would be a witness to the murder."

There; she said it. Murder. April was murdered. Aunt Carrie let out a strangled-sounding gasp.

"Joey will want to know what happened to her mommy. She's very close to her grandmother. Can Carrie see her, bring her home here? April and Joey were living here up until six months ago. Joey will feel safe here with her grandmother. How can we contact social services, or will they contact her grandmother? How do we make this happen?"

As I went into overdrive to get Joey home where she belonged, Aunt Carrie stopped pacing and took control.

She demanded they put her in touch with Joey immediately. I have never seen such determination in my life. It was a challenge that no one could resist.

Detective Myer told her that of course they would find out where Joey was exactly and make sure she would be safely ensconced in her grandmother's home.

I stayed with Aunt Carrie as the detectives took their leave. We went into her kitchen and I put on a pot of coffee. I saw that she had some homemade sweet rolls left over from the other morning and I heated them up in the toaster oven as the coffee dripped into the pot.

I made her sit down at the table and offered her coffee and comfort food, just like she had done for me so many times before. Except my issues weren't nearly as bad as this. Losing a child, no matter at what age, had to be the ultimate sorrow. I was at a loss for words. And for the first time ever, Aunt Carrie was not eating her sweet rolls. Instead, she just sat and drank coffee.

She remained quiet as we sat. There really wasn't anything to say, so I sat with her and tried my best to be totally present.

As she finished her last cup of coffee, she finally looked at me with tears in her eyes and said, "It's strange, but as sudden as this is, I'm not really surprised, you know?"

I did know. It was the unspoken topic between us ever since April went to live by herself with Joey.

"Aunt Carrie, there was nothing you could have done to prevent this. It's not your fault."

"You were always good at reading my mind, MJ. But you and I both know that I could have been more forceful at having her stay at my house."

"Maybe, but these kind of guys never get over a rejection and will wait for the right time no matter how long it takes. I don't know if this could have been prevented. Maybe delayed, but I'm not sure about how it could have been prevented."

"MJ, tell me the truth. Do you think it was Alex?"

I almost told her that I was absolutely sure it was him, but instead said, "To be honest, he was the first person that came to my mind. I think we'll have to wait until they do their investigation. Let's just hope that you get Joey sooner rather than later."

"That poor child, losing her mother at such a young age. How will she ever recover? And to even think that she might have seen or heard something just breaks my heart."

At this point, Aunt Carrie broke down and sobbed into her hands. I went in search of Kleenex and sat next to her at the table, tissue box in hand. I wanted to absorb some of the pain for her, but didn't know how.

I wished for a strong drink sitting there beside her and wondered if she had anything in her house. I was wise not to ask. If she needed something, I'd leave it up to her to ask for it. She didn't.

The day seemed to go on forever and took on a surreal quality. Aunt Carrie made some phone calls to friends and family back in the Midwest. I checked my texts and emails as she did this. I was also able to cancel my clients for the day. I felt relief that I didn't have to see anyone. I knew I wouldn't be able to focus on anything except April's death.

Finally, by the end of the day, at around 5 p.m., Aunt Carrie got a call from the social worker who was in charge of Joey. She was bringing Joey over to see her grandmother.

We both let out a sigh of relief.

Chapter 6

It was a touching reunion. Joey flew into her grandmother's arms and Aunt Carrie hugged her to her ample breast and tried not to weep. I stood and watched, wishing that I had a family that cared that much about each other.

I felt a little hurt that Joey didn't acknowledge me, but also realized that she had just been through a major trauma and I could see that she was falling asleep in her grandmother's arms.

The social worker, Marilyn Parks, was a middle-aged woman with some gray starting to show, who seemed competent and reassuring. However, she did say that when Joey's dad was found, he had the right to take Joey to be with him.

"Even if he's a suspect?" I asked.

"Unless he's being arrested, he's her father and is her next of kin. He has the right to take her. Since there doesn't seem to be any record of abuse toward Joey by him, and he has 50% custody, our hands are tied."

It was unbelievable to me since I knew the true story, but I also knew how the system worked. We'd have to hope and pray that once April was gone, Alex would lose interest in Joey and Aunt Carrie would become her legal guardian.

Aunt Carrie told me to just leave it: for now. Joey was safe with her at the moment and that's all she cared about.

"Where is Alex? Does anyone know?" I asked.

"We and the police are trying to find him," said the social worker. "He's not at his address and isn't answering any of his calls. They go straight to voicemail."

"Doesn't that prove he's guilty? He ran away from the scene of the crime."

"MJ," Aunt Carrie said, "please, not in front of the child. Just leave it for now. There will be time to get these questions answered soon enough. Right now I need to get Joey into her pajamas and to bed. She's already half asleep. Can you get all the details of what happened to Joey while I get her into her Pjs? I have some for her that were left in the laundry. But I'm going to need some more cloths for her from the house. Can someone go and pick them up for me?"

With that she turned to Marilyn Parks for an answer.

"I'm sorry, but they aren't letting anyone in yet. The police will let you know when it's open to you."

With that answer, Aunt Carrie stood and carried little Joey into her bedroom, cooing and soothing her as she went. I could see that Joey was exhausted; her eyelids were drooping. She'd be asleep in no time.

When they were safely out of hearing, I asked the important questions. "What did you tell Joey when you went to pick her up? Was she scared? Did the police interrogate her?"

"No, we got there pretty much right after they had broken in to rescue her. They had her in a blanket and one of the officers was showing her his badge and making funny faces that made her laugh. She didn't seem that upset when I got there, but she did keep asking for her mother."

"What did you tell her?"

I wasn't a child psychologist, so wasn't sure how these things were handled, but I knew that Joey would be suffering from trauma. Just the fact that policeman had to break the door down and she was alone with no one around that she was familiar with would be a trauma, in and of itself.

"We took her to the center downtown and gave her some juice. She wouldn't eat anything, which is understandable. Later, she did eat some cheese and crackers. We had a child psychologist come in who allowed her to play with the toys, so she could see what Joey was dealing with through her play.

"It seems that Joey has had a lot of social interaction because she seemed to adapt well to strangers and was quite verbal. We told her that we were looking for her daddy, but that mommy got hurt and she couldn't see her."

I guess that was going to be as good as it got for the moment. I was grateful that they brought her to her grandmother and the house she had learned to feel safe in.

"How did she react when you told her you were looking for her daddy?"

"She didn't really react at all, but got really quiet. You know, Ms. Lange, I'm not the enemy here. I'm also not the person who's going to be making the final decisions about where Joey will live. There are a lot of moving parts. For all we know, her father has also been hurt. We can't find him and he's not answering his cell. But for now, I can see that Joey is in good hands with her grandmother."

I had to be satisfied with her answer, but was really wanting reassurance that she would not be going with Alex. I wondered where he could have gone. I hadn't for a moment thought he had also been hurt. I was convinced that he was the one who murdered April. I hated that man for how he had treated April and Joey. I had no sympathy at all for him. I have a very negative reaction to any type of abuse and refuse to work with perpetrators. I'm well aware of my bias and I know I could never be impartial if I had to work with someone who was abusive.

I got Marilyn's contact information before she left, then went into the living room and sat vigil in case there was any more news. I also wanted to be available in case Aunt Carrie couldn't sleep and needed someone to be with her.

I knew that once the autopsy was done and April's body was released, Aunt Carrie would have to make arrangements for her burial. I had no idea what her religious beliefs were, or even if she had any. But I knew I'd be there by her side all the way.

I finally dozed off but woke abruptly at 1 a.m. and looked around. I was still alone so I got up and quietly went to peek in on Aunt Carrie and Joey. They were both asleep with Joey cuddled up to Aunt Carrie, a little arm and a leg draped over her grandmother who slept on her back, snoring softly.

I closed the door gently and went back to the sofa where I dialed Big Al.

When he answered, all I could do was cry.

Chapter 7

The smell of coffee woke me and I found myself lying on the sofa with a light quilt covering me. I did not want to wake up. I did not want to greet the day. I did not want to have to see the sorrow on Aunt Carrie's face. And I especially did not want to feel anything about April's murder and how awful it would be for Joey.

I attempted to wet my dry lips with an even dryer tongue and closed my eyes again, trying to go back into the comfortable cocoon of sleep. When I opened my eyes again, I saw little eyes staring at me.

"Hey, Joey."

"Hi, MJ. Do you live here with Nana too?"

Joey had changed from calling Aunt Carrie, Grandma to Nana. She had difficulty saying her R's, so grandma had come out gwamma. Since April called her mother mama, Joey called her Nana, thinking that's what April was calling her. So cute and looking back on it, so innocent and special. I felt a tear slide down my cheek. The thought of this family never being whole again was so painful.

I sat up and reached my arms out to Joey, "Nope, I just had a sleepover last night. Come here, Pumpkin."

Joey giggled and crawled up on to the sofa and said, "Why you call me pumpkin?"

"Oh, I don't know. It just seemed right. Why? You don't like Pumpkin?"

She giggled as I tickled her belly.

I had to remind myself that she was only four years old and didn't experience grief the way adults do. Kids live in the present and at the moment she was being tickled and it was fun for her.

I heard Aunt Carrie bustling around in the kitchen and knew that she'd found a way to stay sane. She was the master at baking comfort food and eating it too. I wasn't going to make her stop. It was good for her.

"Okay, little one, let's go have breakfast with Nana."

Joey jumped off the sofa and still in her pink pajamas with red hearts, she raced into the kitchen and climbed on to her chair. The chair she had used when she and her mother lived with Aunt Carrie. If I didn't know better, it could have been a normal morning with Aunt Carrie cooking and all of us sitting around the table enjoying the food.

We were being served pancakes and scrambled eggs with a side of bacon. It smelled wonderful and my stomach growled. However, when I started to pour syrup on my pancakes, I started feeling faint and knew I wasn't breathing right. I had been holding my breath and felt dizzy.

I gripped the table with my hands and took in a large gulp of air and counted slowly. I took a deep breath in for a count of four, held for a count of four, and exhaled for a count of eight.

Aunt Carrie stood up from the table and walked around to where I was sitting and gave me a hug saying, "It's okay, MJ, I understand. You've been through a lot these past two years. I'm glad you stayed with me last night and I appreciate your loyalty, but I can see this is a big trigger for you. You need to go see your trauma therapist, or go to a meeting, or whatever it is you do."

She was referring to the fact that I killed a man almost two years ago when he tried to strangle me to death, and then the next year, I witnessed a young client of mine use a gun to blow a hole into his mouth to end his life. Yes, I had been through some traumatic stuff, not to mention that as a teenager, I walked in on the aftermath of my father's bloody suicide.

I patted her hand and told her that I'd be okay. This was more important than anything I had gone through.

"MJ, I'm going to need you by my side. I'm counting on you to help me through this. I can't have you starting to drink again. After you get some food into your stomach, I want you to go to a meeting and make an appointment with your therapist. I insist."

"Well, when you put it that way, of course I'll go take care of myself."

I knew she was right. I was in awe at her ability to take command the day after finding out her only daughter was murdered. I decided that I would step up to the plate and do what I knew I had to do in order to keep my sanity.

"I promise, Aunt Carrie. I will take care of *me* today, so I can come and take care of *you*."

I forced the pancakes down my throat, knowing I had to keep my blood sugar up. I washed them down with the bitter coffee that was her trademark. My throat seemed to constrict and the coffee helped the food go down.

After giving Joey a big hug and promising I'd see her later, I left Aunt Carrie's house to go home and take a hot shower. Even though the day was already starting to get hot, I felt chilled to the bone and couldn't stop shaking until I stood under the hot water for what seemed like hours.

When I got out of the shower, I saw that there was still time to catch my AA home meeting. I threw on some shorts and a t-shirt, grabbed my bag and hurried out to the car. I mentally made a plan to call my therapist after the meeting.

I knew the signs of my PTSD. Aunt Carrie was right. I needed help.

Chapter 8

The AA meeting had already begun when I entered. Since I had coffee and pancakes at Aunt Carrie's, I skipped the coffee and almond crescent I usually had and sat in the back as the speaker began to tell her story.

When she finished, I realized that I hadn't heard a word she had said. But I did hear her suggest the topic of the meeting, which was 'overcoming adversity,' and I knew that was the perfect topic for me to share on that morning.

Even though I had been going to meetings for nine months, I had never shared at one. But I felt compelled to share about what happened to April, so I raised my hand up high.

When the speaker called on me, I momentarily couldn't speak. Emotions overtook me and tears came to my eyes as I blurted, "He killed her. Strangled her right outside of her door, leaving Joey alone in the house. He's a monster."

At that point, I broke down and sobbed. I felt someone put their arms around me and say, "It's okay. We're here for you. It's okay. Here, take a Kleenex."

The act of giving me a simple Kleenex for something as egregious as a murder made me look into the woman's kind eyes and I started to laugh hysterically. I could not stop. I shifted once again to big sobs as my entire body shuddered.

Before I knew it, Big Al was leading me outside and walking me around the parking lot. He didn't say a word, but let me alternate between sobbing and laughing. I was talking, but not making much sense.

After a while, when I was able to calm myself down, Big Al looked down at me and searched my eyes for an explanation.

"MJ, what happened?"

"Oh my god, Al, Alex killed April."

He let out a big sigh and then crushed me to his chest and held me there as my body shook uncontrollably. I finally felt the heat of the sun on us and felt claustrophobic with his crushing hug and pulled myself away. I took big breaths of hot, summer air as I looked around for someplace to sit.

Big Al, sensing what it was that I needed, led me to a bench that was up against the church and we sat down together.

"So April's dead." It wasn't a question, but a statement of fact.

"Al, she was found in her back yard, partly sitting up against her back door. Their initial impression is that she was strangled, but we won't know until the autopsy."

"I'm so sorry, MJ."

"But that's not the worst part, Al. Little Joey was left inside the house all by herself, with the doors locked. If it was Alex, he's a monster. What father would kill his daughter's mother and then just leave her there for who knows how long all by herself at age four?"

"How long was she left in the house?"

"I don't really know because we don't know the time of death for April. Joey actually called 911 from her mother's cell phone early in the morning. I don't know what time. The 911 operator had her hold on while she sent someone to her house. The cell phone alerted them to Joey's location, thank god. Otherwise, she could have been there for days before anyone found her."

I gasped as I just realized this and could hardly contain myself at how things could have turned out even more horribly if Joey had been left there alone. Or worse, if Joey opened the door and saw her mother propped up on the door; dead. I couldn't even imagine how terrible that would have been for that child and I shook my head to get rid of that horrifying image.

"MJ, where is Joey now? Is she okay?"

"Yes, she's with Aunt Carrie. They can't find Alex. He's disappeared. Or he's out of town, or he's run away because he murdered April and is hiding. I don't know where he could be unless he's hiding from the police. The social worker told us that they're concerned that maybe Alex was harmed also, but I think he did it."

"Let's not jump to any conclusions, MJ. For now, let's get you settled. Let's come up with a plan for you, okay?"

"But, Al, I haven't even told you the worst part yet."

He looked at me dubiously and I didn't blame him, because what could be worse than a murder?

"The social worker said that because Alex is Joey's next of kin, Joey would be given to him to take care of her. That can't happen. Al, that just can't happen."

"I hear you, MJ. I really do. But let's not get ahead of ourselves. Remember, it's not up to you to decide any of this. You aren't the cops, you aren't Joey's mother, and you really have no control over any of this. As much as you'd like to think you do have control, or as much as you'd like to fix it, you can't. It's not yours to fix."

I took a deep breath and what I had learned in my nine months of going to AA meetings came through and metaphorically hit me over the head. Al was right. None of this was in my control. I couldn't fix this. All I could do was to be present for Aunt Carrie and little Joey.

Aunt Carrie told me she needed me to be there with her for all of what she was going to have to go through. And it was going to be a lot. Especially if Alex was found and took charge of Joey. This was all out of my control. I'm very good at seeing the whole picture when I'm helping my clients, but when it comes to seeing my own issues, I'm pretty blind. I was determined to stay calm and clear for her.

I looked over at Big Al and said, "You know, you're right. Thank you for setting me straight."

After a deep breath, I took his hands in mine and sat there trying to gather strength from him. Even though it was nearly 80 degrees already in the morning, my hands were icy cold. Big Al took them between his and started rubbing them with his warm, enormous paws.

I tried for a smile, but it just wasn't there, so I gave a half-hearted grimace instead.

The AA meeting was over at this point and people started coming out of the church to go to their cars. Nearly all of them stopped for a short time and either gave me a heartfelt hug, or expressed some words of encouragement. I was surprised that no one asked for the specifics. They seemed to sense that Big Al had it under control and probably figured I'd share what happened in the next meeting. But more likely, they realized it wasn't any of their business, the very thing I was trying to learn.

Chapter 9

After making a plan of action for myself with Big Al, I went to my car and before I even started it, I made the call to my trauma therapist and made an emergency appointment with her for later that day. I then looked up another AA meeting I could go to while waiting for my appointment with my therapist. I found one in Santa Monica that was starting in half an hour.

Big Al was concerned that April's murder could trigger my drinking. He wasn't wrong because I was already feeling a strong urge to buy a bottle of vodka and take a few shots, just to take the edge off.

I knew I was in a fragile place, being newly sober. I was aware that any kind of event that I felt incapable of handling could start the drinking. I wasn't stupid; I was just automatically searching out my old way of coping. But I also had some new tools to keep me from using alcohol as my crutch.

While driving to my second meeting of the day, I saw I had a message from Aunt Carrie. She asked how I was coping.

So like her to think of me first, when it was she who just lost a daughter.

I texted her back telling her that I was getting my priorities in order and on my way to another AA meeting, after which I'd be seeing my trauma therapist.

She replied, "Good. So far Joey and I are baking cookies and she hasn't asked too much about her mother yet."

I wasn't looking forward to when that time came. I figured Aunt Carrie would want my input when that happened. I was surprised that Joey wasn't talking about the policemen who broke her door down. It seemed like that would be something Joey would be chatting about. I don't know, maybe she didn't really understand what had happened and was living in the moment; being safe with her Nana.

I asked Aunt Carrie if she'd like me to come over after my therapy session and she immediately responded, "Yes please."

I understood the 'yes please' was a cry for help. I knew Aunt Carrie wouldn't try to impose anything on me, so the fact that she wanted me to come over meant that she was hurting and needed someone to be with her. I was determined to suck it up and be present for her.

After I ended the call to Aunt Carrie, I realized that I hadn't called Franny to tell her what happened. It shocked me because she was usually the first one I would think of when I needed to share, or didn't want to be alone.

It made me sad that we were drifting apart, so I put my earbuds in and made the call.

"Hi, MJ. I was beginning to think that you were ghosting me."

I couldn't answer right away because the truth was that I was putting distance between us and it felt uncomfortable to me. But it also felt like I needed to keep the distance until I could cope with my drinking. She loved the fact that I was getting sober, but it was also a fact that most of the time we had drinks when we got together. We were trying to find a different kind of friendship. I knew that wouldn't happen until I learned to put myself first. Plus, even though she hated my drinking, Franny usually gave me a couple of shots of alcohol whenever there was something going on with me where I felt I couldn't cope. That was a dynamic between us that I hadn't yet broached with her.

Big Al told me that Franny was being an enabler and I knew he was most likely right. I understood alcoholism and all the co-dependent issues. I couldn't be an effective therapist unless I had studied and understood this. It's just that when it came to my own sobriety, it was like I was dumb and dumber.

"No, Franny, I'm not ghosting you. You have to know that Aunt Carrie's daughter, April, was murdered last night, or maybe early this morning. They don't really know exactly when it happened."

"Oh my god, MJ, what happened?"

I filled her in while I drove to my meeting. She immediately told me to come to her place. She told me that she was there for me.

It took a lot from me to tell her no, that I was going to an AA meeting and then my therapist. She insisted that I come after the therapy session, which I again had to decline. I needed to go to be with Aunt Carrie.

I know she felt left out because she kind of hung up on me with a curt, "Okay then, MJ, do what you have to do."

She sounded irritated rather than understanding. She didn't tell me how sorry she was and she knew that I must be really upset. She might as well have just slammed the phone down in my ear, if any of us still had a telephone to do so.

My relationship with Franny weighed heavily on my mind as I entered my second meeting of the day. I recognized some of the people and nodded to them. I still wasn't the hugger type like some of them were, and that suited me just fine. I tried not to think of Franny and her hurt feelings as the meeting began and tried to focus instead on what was being said.

My mind wandered and I kept thinking about what must have happened to April. She must have known the person who killed her because she had stepped outside into her back yard and locked the door behind her. We know this because Joey had been locked in. Based on that, I figured it had to have been Alex.

Where the hell was he anyway? Why couldn't they find him already? Surely, if he did premeditate her murder, he'd have a plan with an alibi and be available. Since he was missing, I figured, it must have been a spontaneous passion killing. Maybe he got angry and didn't mean to kill her, but it happened and he panicked and ran away. This seemed like the most obvious reason they couldn't find him.

It was a mystery. When the meeting came to an end, I was surprised to find myself automatically standing and holding hands as we all recited the Serenity Prayer. I still didn't know it by heart. I kept getting confused about which part was *accept* and which part was *courage*. It was probably because it started out with God, and I didn't believe in God, so there was definitely a resistance there. I mean, how could a loving God let all these terrible things happen?

As I hurried to leave the church where the meeting was being held, I saw a man in my peripheral vision running up to me. I didn't really have time to talk to anyone and quickly unlocked my old VW bug and got in the drivers' side.

A hand reached out to keep me from closing the door. I started to panic until I heard my name being called by a familiar voice.

"MJ, it's me."

Chapter 10

I looked up into Jesse's eyes.

"What. . . what the hell, Jesse." I stammered. I wasn't expecting to see him and looking into those blue eyes, I was transported to our time together—months ago. I had fallen for him and had believed that he was starting to fall for me too.

"Why are you here? Were you at my AA meeting?" I was confused and had a momentary thought that he was following me.

"No, I was not at your AA meeting and did not even know you'd be here. I'm here picking up a friend and saw you come running out. I was surprised to see you, but I'm happy to run into you."

I let out a deep sigh. I wanted so much to invite him for a coffee and talk like old times. He was a good listener and I always felt safe with him. He also had a wicked sense of humor and made me laugh—not an easy thing to do with someone like me who took life so seriously.

"Hey, I have to take my friend home; he lost his license on a DUI, but could we meet up later? Get a coffee or something?"

I wanted to say yes so badly, but I knew it was the wrong thing to do, not just for me but for him too. Besides, I had my therapy appointment and then I needed to be with Aunt Carrie.

Regretfully, I turned him down. He must have noticed how I had hesitated before saying no. He jumped in quickly, asking me if we could meet another day when I wasn't so busy.

I put my hands on the steering wheel and clutched it tightly willing myself to get a grip and just say no. But April's murder was so very fresh on my mind and Jesse was a cop. I thought he would have some insight into what may have happened and how the investigation would be handled. I wanted to help Aunt Carrie as much as I could.

As I sat in the car with Jesse waiting for an answer, I had what I thought was a brilliant idea. "Jesse, remember April, Aunt Carrie's daughter? The woman whose boyfriend was trying to manipulate her into staying with him but she left anyway? You were going to help her move?"

"Yes," he drew the word out as if he were trying to figure out where I was going with this.

"Well, she was murdered early this morning, or late last. Her mother is understandably devastated. April's little girl, Joey, is living with Aunt Carrie now. Things are surreal and they can't find the father. We're worried that if and when they do find him, if they can't pin the murder on him, he'll be able to take Joey, since he's the next of kin. That would just kill Aunt Carrie—and me too."

My words came rushing out and I realized that I was a total mess, barely able to hold it together.

Jesse came in close and pried my hands from the steering wheel, squatting beside me and holding my hands. His eyes were sympathetic and I couldn't keep from crying. I hadn't realized how alone I had been feeling ever since I heard the news this morning.

I let him reach out and wipe the tears from my face as he said, "MJ, I'm so sorry. This is really terrible. I can only imagine what her mother must be going through. How can I help?"

My brilliant idea didn't seem so brilliant after all and I sat in the car feeling the heat of the day warm up the car to an almost suffocating level.

"I was going to ask you to come to Aunt Carrie's house when I would be there tonight, so you could answer questions we might have. But now that I think it through, it's probably a terrible idea."

"No, it's not a terrible idea. I'd love to come over and help if I can, but would your friend feel comfortable with me coming? She just lost her daughter; I don't want to overstep here. She may just need you to be with her tonight. Why don't you ask her what she would like when you get to her place? If it would help, give me a call and I'll come over. Is she the one that lives next door to you?"

I let out a sigh of relief. He was making so much sense. I couldn't be logical because I was still upset about the murder and how Aunt Carrie was feeling. But even more so, I was upset at how little Joey was going to cope with the loss of her mother at such an early age. Especially if she was going to have to live with her father. I knew it would be difficult for Aunt Carrie to get visitation rights as a grandparent in the state of California, if Alex refused her access to Joey. And I was pretty sure Alex would not allow it, and that would kill her.

I thanked Jesse and after reassuring him that I was okay to drive, he closed my door and walked over to the man who must have been his friend with the DUI. I drove off to see my therapist.

Chapter 11

It was good to see my trauma therapist. I had started to see her after I killed the man in self defense almost two years ago. She helped me a lot and I was about to stop seeing her, when that client of mine committed suicide in front of me nine months ago. I decided to continue seeing her, and also made the decision to commit to a life of sobriety.

Eventually, we were only having sessions once a month, but April's murder constituted an emergency. It had the capacity to trigger all of my past trauma. I wanted to make sure I was in a good place in order to support Aunt Carrie, and to do that, I knew I needed this emergency session.

"MJ, good to see you, but I hate the circumstances that have you coming in today. Tell me what happened."

After I went through all the details and my concerns and worries, she asked what I had done to calm myself and then asked my level of anxiety.

I was kind of amazed that from a one to ten anxiety level, I was only experiencing a level of seven. She was impressed and

I have to say, I was too. All the therapy and the AA meetings were obviously helping. I knew if this had happened a year ago, I would have been at level ten and above.

We reviewed a few of the techniques she had taught me and I informed her that I was using the breathing technique the most, along with going to extra meetings and staying in contact with my AA sponsor, Big Al. Then she asked me what control I had in this situation.

I understood how important this question was, so I gave myself time to really think about it.

"Well, I don't have any control over what has already happened. I don't have any control over how Aunt Carrie feels, or how awful it is for her. I have no control over who will ultimately be taking care of little Joey. So obviously, the only thing that I have any control over at all is how I'm going to handle this. I do worry if I'll be able to be strong and supportive for my friend and if I'll be able to sit with her through her pain. The pain of not only losing her daughter, but losing her granddaughter as well unless she is granted custody. But I'm also worried that I'll not take care of my own grief."

"How does that make you feel?"

"Actually, in some weird way, it is a relief to really know that I don't have any control over any of this. I'm so used to trying to fix everything and make things turn out okay. Knowing that this is way out of my ability to fix any of it allows me to set my priorities. I know that the best thing I can do is to be present for my friend, even though I wish I could make it all go away."

The enormity of the situation hit me and I allowed myself to cry with the grief of losing my good friend. I also cried over the fear of losing Joey. I had been so intent on trying to be available for Aunt Carrie, that I hadn't allowed myself to feel my own grief.

"MJ, you've come a long way in these past two years. You should be very proud of yourself. How's the drinking going?"

"I think what you meant to say is 'how is your recovery going?'" I laughed and immediately felt guilty for finding anything funny in the face of what just happened earlier in the morning.

"MJ, it's okay to laugh. You are alive. You didn't die. You survived. April didn't. You have nothing to feel guilty about. You are a survivor. For whatever reason, April wasn't able to fight for her life but it's not your fault. Just like it wasn't your fault when your father chose to end his life."

And there is was. The guilt I had been carrying, and still carry if I were to admit it, since I was sixteen years old. As much as I try to help people and as much as I try to fix everything for everyone, it's never enough. I can never and will never be able to make it right for my dad.

I looked at my therapist with sad eyes and saw the compassion in hers. I logically knew I wasn't responsible for his death, or my client's, or even the murderous Mike Rimichi. But the guilt stayed with me and ate me up inside. I wasn't sure that I'd ever be totally rid of it.

Our time was up and we made another appointment for the following week. I saw that it was close to dinner time. I called Aunt Carrie and asked her if she'd like me to pick up a pizza or some Thai food.

I could hear her call out to Joey to ask if she'd like pizza for dinner and heard a resounding, "Pizza. Yes. Pizza."

So pizza it was. After I placed the order for pick up, I stopped at a 7 Eleven store and picked up some coffee ice cream. It's my favorite, but I also knew that Joey liked it too. I was surprised the first time I offered her some in my apartment almost a year ago and she said yes. I had given her a tiny amount, being sure that a three-year-old would hate coffee ice cream. I had been wrong; she gobbled it up and asked for a BIG scoop.

When I arrived with pizza and ice cream I was greeted with the joyous exuberance of the four-year-old. She was jumping up and down and asking why it took me so long. I handed her the ice cream and told her she could have some after we ate our pizza.

Aunt Carrie followed after Joey and grabbed the pizza from me, telling her granddaughter to put the ice cream in the freezer to keep it from melting. She had one of those freezers that you open from the bottom, so it was easy for a little girl to manage. I knew that Aunt Carrie had popsicles in her freezer, sugar-free, for Joey to have whenever she wanted. I had to laugh at her attempt to keep sugar from Joey because Aunt Carrie baked constantly and had mounds of cookies, brownies, pies, and cakes for all of us to consume.

After we gorged on pizza and ice cream, I could see Joey's eyes starting to close. Aunt Carrie carried her into her bedroom to change her into her pajamas and tuck her in for the night. It seemed early, but I imagined with all the drama and not having her mother around, she was tired and that sleep would be a grateful relief for her.

When Aunt Carrie came back to the kitchen, I had already cleaned up and she said, "MJ, you didn't have to do that. You brought the food."

"I know, but I want to be helpful, Aunt Carrie. Please let me help you."

"Thank you, MJ. Can you go say good night to Joey? She wants a hug from you. I think she's missing her mother."

Entering Joey's room, I saw that she had a night light on that showed colorful kittens dancing as the light apparatus turned. It was clever and made the room feel safe and cozy.

"Good night, my princess," I said as I sat down on her bed next to her and started rubbing her back.

"MJ?"

"Yes, Sweetie?"

"When is my mommy coming back?"

I shouldn't have been surprised by the question but I was momentarily speechless. "What has your Nana told you, Honey?"

"I haven't asked her."

"Oh? Why not?"

"Every time I talk about my mommy, she gets sad."

"I see."

We really can't hide things from children. They are so perceptive. But she asked a question and the only answer I had would crush her and I didn't feel it was my place.

I'm ashamed to admit it, but I deflected by picking up the book she had next to her on her bed and told her that I was going to read her to sleep. By the time I finished, she was asleep. I was left with my feelings of guilt at not being truthful with her.

When I returned to the kitchen, Aunt Carrie was sitting at the table with her head in her hands, moving her head back and forth. I sat and waited, not sure if I should touch her, talk, or just leave her alone. I opted to just sit quietly and wait for her to give me a clue.

As the minutes ticked by, I saw that her shoulders started to shake and I knew that she wasn't able to keep the grief in anymore, nor did she need to. She had kept her face cheerful and interested in whatever Joey had to say, but when Joey was no longer with her, she started to fall apart. And who could blame her? I was surprised she lasted as long as she did.

When she finally looked up at me, tears streaming down her face, I reached out and gently took her hands in mine and said, "I am so, so sorry."

This started another torrent of tears and I sat holding her hands until she couldn't cry anymore.

I got up and helped her to her feet. I led her into her bedroom and had her lie down on the bed. I took her shoes off and then covered her with a light blanket.

I sat beside her until she went to sleep, feeling a hateful need for vengeance against whomever took April from us; and I was pretty sure it was Alex.

Chapter 12

Leaving Aunt Carrie to get some badly needed sleep, I left the door open and took my vigil on her sofa in the living room, knowing I'd be able to hear either one of them if they called out in the night.

I was exhausted too. I rested my head on the back of the sofa and closed my eyes. Just as I was drifting off, I felt my phone buzz in my pocket.

It was Jesse. I had completely forgotten that he offered to come and talk to us about how the investigation would most likely go.

"Hi, Jesse."

"Where are you?"

"I'm at Aunt Carrie's house. Both she and Joey are asleep already. They were exhausted. I'm sorry, I never got the chance to ask her if she wanted you to talk to her about procedure. You were right that she may not be up for this yet and it didn't seem appropriate to do so tonight; maybe tomorrow or in a couple of days. Let's see how it goes. But thanks for offering your expertise. I appreciate it."

"No problem, MJ. Just know that I'm here for you guys."

I wanted to tell him to come over anyway. I wanted to tell him that I needed him. I was in a very vulnerable place and he was being so kind.

"Okay, Jesse. Thank you, I'll let you know if she would like help from you. I think the next couple of days are going to be very busy. The autopsy should be completed soon and I assume the detectives will want more information. Also, there will need to be preparations for a funeral, or whatever it is that Aunt Carrie will want to do. There is no family out here and since Alex kept April so isolated, there won't be many people who would want to come, so I'm not sure she'll even have a funeral."

"I'd like to come, MJ."

"Really?"

"Yes, please let me know if and when and where it will be."

"Okay, that's really kind of you." But I wasn't sure I'd actually let him know.

"MJ, I know I was a jerk for the way I let you down. I feel like a heel and have so many regrets. But whatever you may think of me, it won't change the way I feel about you. Look, I know I have no right to be telling you this at this point, but I really do care about you, and if there is anything I can do to help out, I will. No strings attached. I promise."

I knew that and that's why I had gotten so fond of him. He was a study in contrasts. He was hard core cop, but was okay with bending the rules if he thought it was for the good and would take bad guys off the street. He was also kind, but obtuse at times being totally unaware of how his actions affected others. Like him not letting me know that his wife asked him to try again until he was forced to. I doubted that he really understood how painful it had been for me when he went back to her.

There really wasn't anything to be gained by rehashing any of it and there was nothing in it for me if I were to stay connected to him. So I thanked him again for his offer and said good-bye.

"MJ, wait."

"Yes?"

"I know I don't have any right, but could we just get together and talk?"

"Talk about what?"

"I don't know, just talk. I'm so confused."

"Are you still living with your wife?"

"Yes, but it's not a real marriage anymore. It's a marriage for the kids."

"Does she know that?"

"What do you mean?"

"Does she agree that it's just a marriage of convenience to keep the family together for the kids?"

"I'm trying, but I just don't have the same feelings for her that I used to have."

"Does she still have feelings for you?"

I heard a deep sigh.

"I guess I have my answer."

"MJ, you don't understand."

"Here's what I understand, Jesse. I understand that you're really trying to make a marriage work for the sake of the kids. I admire that. I really do. What I don't admire is trying to make a marriage work based on lies."

"I never lied to her."

"But you aren't telling her that you don't have the same feelings for her anymore. It's a lie by omission, and is that fair to her? Is it fair to you?"

What I didn't ask, was if it was fair to me. I felt like I was talking to a client instead of a man I had fallen in love with.

"What would you have me do?"

I could hear the anguish in his voice and said, "I can't answer that for you, Jesse. You have to figure that one out on your own. I have strong feelings for you, but I can't be meeting up with you as long as you're a married man. I won't do that to her and I won't do it to me. I won't ask you to choose between us, or give you an ultimatum. I won't do that. But what I will do is tell you to not call or contact me until or rather when you have decided that your marriage is over and the divorce is final."

There was another long pause and I almost hung up, thinking he had.

"I understand, MJ. I do. But I am still available for your friend. And I mean it. Please let me help."

"Thank you, Jesse. You're a good man."

After we finished the call, I sat on the sofa and realized there was no more fatigue. In fact, I was feeling wired and I hadn't even had any caffeine. I couldn't leave Aunt Carrie alone because she might wake up at any moment and need something; or Joey may wake up.

I dreaded when Joey would finally realize that her mother was not coming back. Her current experience is that she's having a fun sleepover with her beloved Nana. But what's going to happen when she wants to go home?

She never talked about the police coming and breaking down the door. That was very strange. It was very early in the morning and she may have confused reality with her dream state. I didn't know for sure. I'm not a child psychologist and have never worked with children, although I have worked with a few teenagers in the past and I did not enjoy it. The only clients I was willing to see were adults. Yes, they had childhood trauma, but they had an adult mind. Most of them did, at any rate.

I got up off of the sofa and started pacing around Aunt Carrie's living room. I hoped that the autopsy would be done by the morning or the next day and I hoped that would lend some finality to how April died. The hope would be that she died of a stroke or heart attack, or an undiagnosed aneurysm. What a relief that would be; but I wasn't very hopeful. The detectives seemed pretty sure it was strangulation.

And where the hell was Alex, I wondered? No one turns their phone off, or just doesn't answer if they're innocent. *It had to be him, didn't it?*

Chapter 13

I found myself, once again waking up to little eyes peering up at me. I must have fallen asleep sitting up because my neck was at an awkward angle as I opened my eyes to Joey staring at me.

I winced as I tried to move my neck into its regular position.

"You hoot?" My brain had to translate that a four-year-old meant "hurt". She still had trouble with her R's.

"I'm okay, Joey. I slept sitting up and my neck fell over and is causing me some pain. Isn't that silly of me?"

She laughed and jumped off the sofa and ran into the kitchen where I could smell coffee and bacon. Aunt Carrie was already up and preparing breakfast for us. I realized I was hungry. I stood up and adjusted my neck slowly, stretching it from side to side to loosen it up to where I could turn my head again without too much pain.

In the kitchen, I saw Aunt Carrie. She was fully dressed in fresh clothes and her hair was still wet from her shower. Her eyes were red from crying, but she put on a happy face for both of us. Except she didn't fool me at all since I noticed her smile did not reach her eyes.

"Good morning, Aunt Carrie," I went up to her and drew her into a warm hug, or at least I hoped she felt it as a comfort.

She hugged me back and we stood there for a moment, neither one of us wanting to let go. Then Joey piped up, "I'm hungwe, Nana. I want bacon, bacon, bacon."

Both of us laughed at her singsong voice demanding her bacon. Aunt Carrie told me to sit down. Joey had already climbed on to her chair and had her napkin tucked into her pajama top under her chin.

"I wish you'd let me help you, Aunt Carrie. I should be the one making breakfast for you, not you making me breakfast."

"MJ, you know me better than that. Cooking for the two of you is helping. It keeps me preoccupied. Pour yourself some coffee while I scramble the eggs. It will just be a moment before everything is ready. You can butter the toast when it pops up. That would be a great help."

We prepared and ate breakfast in silence. At least Joey and I ate. Aunt Carrie picked at her food. I've never seen Aunt Carrie not eat with gusto. I knew she was having a terrible time and who could blame her?

"Aunt Carrie, you have to eat." I said gently. "Today you'll most likely get more information and maybe even need to make funeral arrangements. You'll have a lot of questions for the detectives. You need to keep your strength up."

"I know, MJ. I just don't have an appetite. I keep worrying about J-o-e-y. I keep wondering if they'll find A-l-e-x and he'll t-a-k-e her. Just the thought of it makes me s-i-c-k."

Since Joey was sitting at the table with us, she spelled out the names and words, hoping that Joey wouldn't figure out what we were talking about. She's a smart little girl for her age and I wouldn't be surprised is she knew how to spell her name, but she didn't seem to react to what her grandma said.

Since I didn't have a very big private practice yet, I didn't really need to rearrange anything and was able to stay with Aunt Carrie and Joey for the day. I had decided to quite my practice after watching my client shoot himself nine months ago, but then changed my mind and resumed a few months ago, when I finally was able to stop drinking for more than a week or so.

I did, however, need a shower. I left them alone while I made my way back to my flat and hurriedly showered and changed into shorts and a t-shirt. It was going to be another hot day and I wanted to keep as cool as I could since neither Aunt Carrie nor I had air-conditioning.

When I got back to Aunt Carrie's house, she had already received a call from Detective Myer. She told Aunt Carrie that the autopsy results were back and she and Detective Dunham were on their way over to her house and should be there any minute.

"How are you holding up, Aunt Carrie?"

"It's like I'm sitting on pins and needles. I'm so glad you're here. I wonder if you could take Joey for a walk or to your place while I talk to the detectives."

"Of course, whatever you need." Although I was aching to be with Aunt Carrie to be able to help her ask the questions that needed to be asked, I also knew that Joey should not be there to hear what they were going to be saying about her mother.

"MJ, you are a godsend. What would I do without you?"

"I'm just glad I can be here. But remember to ask them about Alex." We weren't spelling words anymore because Joey had gone into her old room where some of her toys remained and was playing by herself.

"I know, MJ. The main thing is to first of all find out how she died. If I could make wishes come true, I would want it to be some undiagnosed illness where she died suddenly and in peace. But I don't think that's what the autopsy will say."

We then heard the doorbell ring letting us know that the detectives had arrived. I was hoping that Joey would be blissfully playing in the back room, so I could stay and hear what they had to say. But true to form, she came running into the living room to see who it was.

When she saw the detectives, her face went from joy to immediate sadness and she said, "I thought it was my mommy. When is she going to come and get me?"

Aunt Carrie and I exchanged a look of heartfelt sorrow. Neither one of us spoke for a while until Detective Myer said, "Is there someplace where we can talk in private?"

That was my cue to turn to Joey and invite her to my house where, I told her, I had gotten another stuffed bear. I had replaced the cockeyed bear Joey had commandeered when she first visited my office with another one. I wondered where the cockeyed bear was. Probably in the house where she had been living with her mother. I turned to Aunt Carrie and the detectives and asked the vital question, "When will the house be released so we can get Joey's things?"

Detective Myer shrugged her shoulders and said it was difficult to say, but that they would try and get someone to come with us so we could pick up the necessary clothes and toys that Joey would need to feel comfortable.

I thanked her and then reached down for Joey's hand and said brightly, "Come Joey, let's go see my new bear. Maybe we can take her on a walk. Would you like that?"

She reluctantly took my hand. It was obvious she knew she was being put off about her mother, but what else could we do? It wasn't up to me to talk to her about her mother and Aunt Carrie needed to talk to the detectives.

When we got to my office and I took the bear down from her perch on the bookshelf, Joey was not excited at all.

"Hey, Joey, this bear doesn't have a name yet. Would you like to pick a name for her?"

"I guess."

I knelt down to her level and started talking to her as if the stuffed bear was talking, "Hi, Joey, I don't have a name yet. I really need a name. What should it be?"

Joey just looked at the bear and then turned from it and climbed up on my sofa and curled up in a ball. She was clearly not going to be pacified. Maybe the detectives coming to the door triggered her memory of yesterday when the police broke her door down and rescued her.

I wasn't sure what to do, so I said, "Joey, is there anything you'd like to ask me?"

She looked up at me and then turned her head away and said as huge tears formed in her eyes, "I want my mommy."

I sat down beside her and cautiously took her and sat her on my lap, enveloping her in my arms.

"Of course you do, Honey."

"I want my mommy." Her voice was getting louder.

I rocked her back and forth and attempted to absorb her pain, but I knew there wasn't anything I could say or do that would ever fix the loss of her mommy. I felt my own tears running down my face and wished that Aunt Carrie would hurry up with the detectives. Joey needed some kind of explanation and I wasn't the person to give it to her.

I held her as she cried out over and over that she wanted her mommy. I could feel the tension in my own body from not knowing the right thing to do for her.

I thought about distracting her, but I knew that wasn't the right thing to do. I'd witnessed the denial of childhood pain enough in my adult clients. As hard as it was for me to sit and hold Joey as she felt her devastating loss, I knew that trying to talk her out of it, or making her feel wrong for feeling so deeply, or trying to distract her would be worse. Her mother was dead. She was never coming back and I felt that Joey was finally starting to understand that. There were too many hush-hush words and too much weirdness going on around her. I'm sure she sensed something was terribly wrong, no matter how hard we tried to keep it normal for her.

My hate for Alex grew as I held this poor sobbing child.

Chapter 14

After what seemed like hours, Joey finally fell asleep in my arms and I placed her on the sofa, covering her with a light blanket. I then searched for my phone and texted Aunt Carrie to see if she was finished with the detectives. I was dying to know what the autopsy said and if they had any word about the whereabouts of Alex.

She responded immediately, telling me that the detectives had just left and I could bring Joey back.

There was no way I was going to wake that little bundle of sorrow, so I informed her grandma that she had been crying for her mother and fell asleep. I asked her if I could call her so we could talk on the phone.

When she answered, I moved away from Joey and went into my bathroom, leaving the door open in case she woke up.

Aunt Carrie told me that the autopsy clarified she was strangled by what appeared to be a wide, flat piece of cloth or leather, most likely a belt.

No Witnesses

I told her that I was so very sorry, and then asked if the detectives had any clues, or evidence of who could have done it. I was actually asking if they had evidence that Alex had done it.

The detectives told Aunt Carrie that whoever did it was most likely someone she knew because she had opened the door and gone outside to meet with him. However, she had also locked the door behind her, which indicated to me that she must not have trusted the person enough to invite him into her house.

They had recreated what they thought had happened for Aunt Carrie, since she had insisted she wanted to know. They told her that they believed that the killer had come from behind, wrapping the belt around her neck tightly and then quickly lifting her up in the air where she wouldn't have any leverage against her attacker. Since there was no sign of a struggle, they believed it came as a surprise to her and she didn't have time to react. They believed that the killer was either quite a bit taller than April, or he had been standing behind her on the steps leading into her house when she was facing away from him.

They had no explanation of why she had locked the door, or how the killer had gotten behind her while she was facing away. Aunt Carrie told me that they were assuming it was a man because of the strength it would have taken to so completely have taken her by surprise creating a situation where she had no ability to fight back.

"Did you ask them about Alex?"

"I did and they still have not found him. But, MJ, they also don't have any evidence that says it was him."

That was such a bummer. Who on earth could have had it out for April if it wasn't Alex?

"Aunt Carrie, did April say anything to you about dating again, or meeting anyone that was pursuing her?"

"The detectives asked me the same question, MJ, and I'm pretty sure she wasn't seeing anyone. She had told me that she was done with men after being with Alex. She was afraid she might get into another relationship that wasn't good for her and wanted to be sure she healed from the one with Alex before she started dating again. Plus, she was being very protective of Joey. She did not want Joey to be in any kind of danger from another man. She felt Alex was already enough danger for Joey and didn't need any more drama."

"Yes, I can understand that."

"Also, MJ, she was so busy defending herself and Joey from Alex that she didn't have any time with work and childcare to even date. It wouldn't have made sense."

"Hmmm. Yes, I can see that. Was there anyone else that she knew at work or from any place else who was threatening her, or stalking her, or acting weird around her?"

"As far as I know there wasn't anyone at work that she was afraid of or was bothering her; no."

"If it wasn't Alex, then there had to be someone else that she knew well enough to open her door and meet them outside. Was there anyone, like a gardener, or fix it man who may have taken a liking to her and maybe she rejected them? Anyone at all?"

Here I was again, trying to solve a murder mystery. Big Al and Franny would both tell me that it wasn't my job to solve it and to let the police do their job. But as a psychotherapist, my job was always to solve the mystery of what happened that caused my clients so much emotional pain. It was difficult for me to just let it go. I needed to know who snuffed out the life of a young mother, leaving a precious four-year-old child motherless. How could I let this go?

"You know, MJ, you might be on to something. As you were talking, it occurred to me that April did mention that there was a young man who lived a few houses down the street from her. He was in his later teens, around seventeen or eighteen. She had told me that she had befriended him a few months ago because he had opened up to her about some things that had happened to him when he was younger. As I recall, he had been bullied at school and no one had done anything about it. Not his parents and not the teachers. He was still carrying resentments about what happened."

"Did he know April was a teacher's aide?"

"I don't know, MJ. April told me about him when we were chatting one day when the topic of bullying came up. I think she was trying to get him to go see the school counselor about it, but he was resisting it."

I could see how a young man with a lot of resentment against the school authorities might take it out on someone like April. April was such a sweet woman and she would have tried to help him. She wouldn't have been afraid to open the door to him. Maybe he had come late at night after drinking or something like that and when they were alone in the backyard, something she said or did may have triggered his anger and he snapped and killed her.

But even if someone else killed her, where was Alex? Surely, he would have seen the news of the murder, or at the very least, needed to contact her in order to let her know he wasn't available to pick Joey up for his time with her.

"Aunt Carrie, you need to tell Detective Myer about this young man. They need to investigate everyone, right? I mean, as much as I hate to admit it, maybe it wasn't Alex. He had never hurt April physically before. That's not his style, right? He was more a sadistic manipulator who got joy in making her life miserable and loving the control he had over her."

I could hear Aunt Carrie crying on the other end of the phone and it hurt me to listen to it. I just let her cry, as I had let Joey cry for her mommy. It was difficult to hear her pain and I began to imagine going out for a drink—a big shot of vodka. But there was no way I was going to leave Joey and Aunt Carrie alone. That thought helped me hang on to my sobriety.

When Aunt Carrie finally stopped crying, she let out a big sigh and started talking about practical matters. They had told her they would be releasing the body the next day and they needed to know what funeral home to release it to.

"Aunt Carrie, have you thought at all about any of this? I mean, do you want to get a casket and have a viewing of April? Do you want a place that does everything for you, or do you just want a small gathering at your home? Maybe some people from her school would want to come and pay respects? Would you like to discuss all of this with me, or with a funeral director? I could come with you."

"I haven't given it any thought at all, MJ. I still think she's going to come walking into my house to get Joey and make plans with me for Sunday brunch. What am I going to do?"

I realized that I needed to take charge, she wasn't up to the task of all of this. I knew I needed to go with her to plan either a cremation or a burial and either a funeral or a small home gathering. But I couldn't do all of this with her and still take care of Joey. We needed help.

"Aunt Carrie, I'm going to call Franny and ask her if she could take care of Joey today and tomorrow while you and I make arrangements for April."

"Okay," she replied meekly. It hurt to hear her give in, but she needed help. She needed someone else to take charge to help her navigate through all the decisions that had to be made.

"One more thing, Aunt Carrie, and it pains me to bring it up, but Joey was crying and asking for her mother before she finally fell asleep. We're going to have to deal with that when she wakes up. I don't think we can put it off any longer. She's finally starting to understand that her mother isn't around and she's sensing something isn't right."

This started another torrent of tears and I waited patiently for her to be able to talk again.

"MJ, what am I going to say to Joey about her mother? I don't know if I can even talk to her about it. I can't bear to see her little life shatter in front of me. Can you help me?"

"Don't worry, Aunt Carrie, you'll know what to say when the time is right. You know her as well as you knew your daughter. You love them both and you'll be strong enough to handle all the anger and all the sorrow that Joey will throw at you. I know you and I have faith that you'll be able to do this. And I'll be right there, helping you. You know I love Joey like she were my own."

"Thank you, MJ."

"I love you, Aunt Carrie."

Chapter 15

After calling Franny and asking her if she could look after Joey while Aunt Carrie and I went to make funeral arrangements, I sat beside Joey again and watched her little innocent face as she slept. I was glad that sleep was preventing her from feeling all the bad that was happening to her little life.

I was also worried that she might not want to stay with Franny. She knew Franny somewhat and was interested in Franny's colorful long fingernails. At one encounter, Franny had allowed her to paint her own nails with some of her polish. Franny was a fun loving-person and got along with everyone, young and old, so I hoped that she would be a ready distraction for Joey while Aunt Carrie and I went to take care of April.

I dreaded having to be around when Aunt Carrie told Joey that her mommy was not coming back. I just didn't want to have to deal with that. I had no experience in talking to children about something so final.

Franny got to my place a little after Joey woke up. Joey didn't seem as worried about her mother as she had been before she cried and went to sleep.

I needn't have had to worry about Franny. She brought a large bag of nail polish and various shades of lipstick and eye shadow, which maybe wasn't so appropriate for a four-year-old. But she also brought hair ribbons and various kinds of barrettes for little girls. Not to mention necklaces and bracelets that shimmered and glittered. She must have stopped off at the store on her way to my place. She really knew the way to a little girl's heart.

Joey's eyes got big as Franny pulled out one thing more interesting to her than the last. Joey was enthralled. Franny couldn't have done a better job of throwing colorful girl's stuff at Joey. I knew they were going to get along just fine, but I left instructions to call me or Aunt Carrie the minute Joey started asking about her mother, just in case. Franny is a lot of things, but I didn't think she'd be able to handle Joey asking about her mother. I told her to tell Joey that she didn't know where her mother was, but when her Nana came back, she could talk to her about it.

Having settled Franny and Joey, I left them painting nails and fashioning their hair and ran over to Aunt Carrie's. She was on her cell phone when I arrived, so I waited patiently for her to finish.

When she ended the call, she looked at me and said, "They have released April and I have called a mortuary service to help with the cremation. They will prep the body so we can see her before they cremate her. I need to get some clothes over to them so they can dress her for the viewing. I need to see her.

That's the only way I'll know she's really gone. I want to touch her, talk to her, tell her I'll take good care of her baby. I need to promise her that I won't let Alex have her."

I didn't know how on earth she could keep a promise like that, but I didn't disagree. I asked her when we needed to get an outfit for April to the mortuary, and when we'd be able to view April. I almost said, 'the body', but caught myself just in time. April was not just a body. She had been a daughter, a mother, a beloved teacher's aide. And she was a good friend to me. I would really miss her. I didn't have time to mourn her for me, yet. I was too busy trying to be there for Aunt Carrie and Joey.

I guessed there would be paperwork and things that would delay releasing April, but they told Aunt Carrie that she'd be ready by tomorrow afternoon. I asked her if she was going to let Joey see her mom. I didn't know what was appropriate. Based on my own experience, I thought it might not be such a bad idea, but didn't want to impose my experience on her.

I remember my mother taking me to see my grandfather after he died. I was four years old. She lifted me up to see him and I remember thinking that it didn't look like him. I don't recall being upset about it and in a weird way, it had made sense to my four-year-old self. But, then again, it was my grandpa and not my mother.

There's a lot written about children going to funerals, and/or viewing an open casket. There are pros and cons. I couldn't tell her what to do, but the question had to be asked.

One thing I did know was that Joey had to be told that her mother had died and wouldn't be coming back. Aunt Carrie couldn't keep putting that off. Joey would be asking about her mother again and probably sooner than later.

"Aunt Carrie, you have to tell Joey that her mother's not coming back. She has the right to know. I don't think you can keep it from her any longer. I think you need to do it today."

"Ach, MJ, I know. I've been worrying about how to tell her the moment I heard that April was killed. I haven't the stamina to break that little girl's heart. I'm not sure what to tell her." She looked at me, her eyes pleading. "What am I going to tell her?"

I looked away for a moment because I didn't have a clue what she should say, but then I tried to detach myself from the situation and pretend that it was a client who was having this dilemma. I always seem to be able to come up with something for my clients; something to empower them to figure things out for themselves.

"Aunt Carrie, I think you'll find the words when it's time to tell her. Just listen to your heart and come from a loving place. You love April and you have nothing but love for Joey. You aren't hurting her. You aren't the one who left her motherless and you without a daughter. You had no control over what happened and you don't have any control over how Joey's going to react."

I could see her shoulders relax and I knew I had said something that would help her when the time came.

"Just remember, you are coming from a place of your own sorrow and you and Joey will share that pain. You can both be a comfort to each other as the days and months pass. You still have each other. Joey adores you. She feels safe and loved by you. She will be sad that her mother isn't here and she will mourn her, as you will. And you will both survive."

What I didn't say is, unless Alex gets ahold of Joey.

Chapter 16

I called Detective Myer to ask for someone to meet us at April's house. We needed to pick out an outfit for her, along with clothes and toys that Joey would need. I drove Aunt Carrie to April's house to wait for someone to let us in and supervise us. They needed to make sure we didn't do anything that would compromise the investigation.

I thought it was ridiculous because the murder took place outside in the backyard. What could possibly be in the house that they'd need to preserve? But I wasn't in charge so kept calm in order for Aunt Carrie to feel secure.

When we were let in, the place seemed very quiet. I had been to April's house several times. But it was different with an active four-year-old. There was always noise from her chatter, or some video or cartoons playing, or music; a household filled with life. As we entered it felt like a silent tomb.

I encouraged Aunt Carrie to focus on what needed to be done. I told her there would be plenty of time after the house was released for her to take care of all of April's belongings. I encouraged her to not think about all of that until later and to just pick out an outfit for April. I told her that I'd help her grab stuff for Joey.

Aunt Carrie went into April's room, and I went into Joey's. I saw the cockeyed bear I had given her when we first met sitting in the middle of her bed and my memory went to the precious time when things were better and Joey had been excited to get that damn bear. The bear seemed to leer at me, but I picked it up anyway, knowing Joey would want it.

After stuffing clothes and toys into the bag I had brought for Joey's things, I went to see if Aunt Carrie had finished picking out April's outfit.

I found her sitting on April's bed with different outfits held tightly in her hands, her face blotchy from crying.

"Aunt Carrie, I have Joey's things. Have you been able to choose something for April?"

She sat motionless, clutching April's clothes. I walked over to her and put my hand on her shoulder. When that didn't get her attention, I sat down beside her and sat quietly beside her.

The officer who had accompanied us into the house stood nervously at the door. I wanted to scream at him to leave us alone. Couldn't he see this poor woman was beside herself with grief? Nothing was ever going to be the sane for her again; nothing.

After sitting together for some time, the officer finally let out some kind of noise that indicated we needed to finish our business and leave.

I took the three outfits from Aunt Carrie's hands and told her that we could take all of them with us and she could decide later. She let me take the items and then let me start to lead her out of the bedroom, but then she stopped and turned around, looking confused until I saw her focus on something on the bed.

She extricated herself from me and walked back to the bed and took what looked like a homemade quilt folded neatly at the end.

"She'll need this to keep warm," she said.

"Yes, of course," I humored her. In death, nothing made sense. April was still alive to her and being a good mother, she wanted to make sure April would stay warm. I understood that she couldn't decide which outfit to pick for April, even though it didn't really matter. No one but us was going to even see her in it. But this was the last motherly thing that Aunt Carrie would ever be able to do for her daughter.

That thought got me crying. I knew Aunt Carrie would never be the same, just like I was never the same after my father committed suicide. And just like after my husband Gideon died on the operating table, and just like after my young client shot himself.

Even with all the losses I had encountered, the loss of a child and the grief of her mother seemed way beyond the kinds of grief I had experienced. I hadn't had a close relationship with my own mother and I was already a teenager when my father took his life. I couldn't actually relate personally to what Aunt Carrie and Joey were feeling, but having seen how close they were and all the love and hope that came from Aunt Carrie toward those two, it seemed so unfair and so very wrong. How could this have happened?

We went to the funeral home to drop off an outfit for April. When we parked in the parking lot, we sat and stared at the three outfits Aunt Carrie had in her arms. I didn't want to rush her so said, "Take your time. There is no rush. All three of them are nice. Is there one in particular that April loved, or that she wore more than the others? Did she have a favorite color?"

I was trying to be helpful, but I could see that I was merely overwhelming her and so I sat still and kept quiet.

At that moment I hated Alex with a passion. Taking April was despicable and I couldn't wait for the police to arrest him. I wanted him to rot in prison.

After a long time, Aunt Carrie let out a deep sigh and said, "I don't suppose it will really matter which outfit she wears, will it?"

It was a rhetorical question, so I did not reply.

She grabbed the purple one and threw the other two into the back seat where we had placed the quilt and opened her door to get out. Her extra weight made it difficult for her to get out of the car and I hurried around to help her. She slapped my hands away from her and said, "Stop hovering, MJ, I'm not handicapped. I can do it myself."

Even though I knew it was an angry reaction that wasn't really about me, it still stung. I had never seen her act this way, especially toward me, and I was a little unsure how to proceed. I backed off and muttered, "Of course you can. I didn't mean any offense."

"I'm sorry, MJ, I just want to get this over with. Can you grab the quilt from the back for me please?"

Just like that, she was her old kind self and I wanted to weep. I wanted her to scream out loud, tear her hair out, and curse Alex. It was such a surreal situation. Here we were taking clothes into a mortuary where they were going to fix a young woman to look good for a few hours before they incinerated her.

I looked up at the few clouds floating in the sky and felt the scorching sun on my face and realized that the rest of the world went on as if this tragedy hadn't happened. I wished that I was back in my little apartment drinking a second cup of coffee as I waited for a client, safe and secure in my little world, far away from murder and grief.

I opened the back door and retrieved the quilt as Aunt Carrie made her way to the door of the funeral home.

When we entered, I saw that It was what one would expect a funeral home to be. There was the sickening smell of carnations, and the thick carpets absorbed the sound so there was a hush and quiet about everything in the place.

We were greeted by a well-dressed woman. She was dressed simply in a dark navy blue dress with low black pumps. She wore a single strand of pearls and small pearl earrings barely seen through her short curly hair that came down to her earlobes.

She asked how she could help and then directed us into a small private room. The place looked expensive and I felt that they were going to take advantage of Aunt Carrie's sorrow, so I was on full alert in order to protect her.

An elderly gentleman came in and solemnly shook Aunt Carrie's hand and sat down across from us.

He seemed to know why we were there and asked if the outfit Aunt Carrie held in her hands was the outfit she wanted April to be dressed in. He called her April, as if she was still alive. His voice was soothing and he seemed to be genuinely concerned with helping us.

He gently lifted the dress from Aunt Carrie's hands and, looking at the quilt I had brought, asked if we would want the quilt back after the viewing. That seemed to shock Aunt Carrie and she looked at me uncertainly.

"Aunt Carrie, what does the quilt mean to you? Would you like to have it as a keepsake, or to give to Joey? It's up to you."

I turned to the gentleman with my questions. "Does Aunt Carrie have to make up her mind right now, or can she have a little time to t think about it? If she does want the quilt back, can she take it after the viewing?"

"Of course, you don't have to make up your mind right now. You can certainly wait until after the viewing this afternoon and evening."

"Oh, I thought that the viewing wouldn't be until tomorrow."

There was an awkward pause before he went on, "I'm so sorry for the confusion; would you like to hold off until tomorrow?"

I looked at Aunt Carrie who shook her head no. She wanted it done as soon as possible.

"I am under the impression that the viewing will just be for close family?"

I looked at Aunt Carrie and she nodded almost imperceptibly.

"Yes," I said for her, "it will most likely be just us. Her family all live in the Mid-west and I don't believe anyone will be coming. Isn't that right, Aunt Carrie?"

Again, she nodded as before.

"Very good," he went on, "will you be wanting a formal funeral, or any kind of keepsake?"

This brought a response from Aunt Carrie, "No funeral; just a cremation with a viewing later today for us. What do you mean, a keepsake?"

"We have various types of urns for the ashes you can pick out. Depending on what type of urn you'd like will affect the cost of the cremation. If you don't wish an urn, we can put the ashes in a wooden box for you, or if you don't wish to keep the ashes or take them with you, there is no extra charge.

He then hurried on with more information. "Plus, we also have jewelry or other types of memorials where we can put a small amount of the ashes. There are also memorials that do not include the ashes. It's up to you. I could show you a brochure if you'd like."

I thought Aunt Carrie, being very practical, would reject any of these keepsakes. I was surprised when she asked to see the brochure.

He reached over to a table I hadn't noticed before and took two of them, handing one to each of us.

I must confess, the photos of these keepsakes were lovely and I was tempted to get one for myself, they were so beautiful. Then I looked at the price and my breath caught. I looked over at Aunt Carrie, who was studying the brochure and running her fingertips over the photos. There was a small smile on her face and I knew she was going to buy something.

She chose two cremation necklaces in sterling silver with the Tree of Life pattern and asked that "Love Forever" be engraved on the back of each one. I guessed one was for her and one was for Joey. The necklace was beautiful with an abalone shell background for the silver tree. The description stated that Tree of Life relates to Eternal Life, which is a form of immortality or reincarnation. I felt that the engraved words appropriately and lovingly spoke to this sentiment.

She then chose an urn to hold the ashes. It was made of purple pearl, purple being April's favorite color and had 'In Loving Memory for my daughter and Joey's mother, April' engraved toward the bottom.

Again, she rejected a funeral, saying that we were just going to have a small gathering at her home on Sunday.

I hadn't known about her plans until that moment, but it was fitting for both Aunt Carrie and April.

Since Sunday was looming in three days, I knew we were going to have to tell Joey that her mother was not coming back that same day. Also, we needed to decide if Joey would be coming with us to the viewing of her mother.

It was all so complicated, not knowing the proper thing to do with Joey. She was only four years old, but she also deserved to be a part of this, didn't she?

Chapter 17

When we got back to Aunt Carrie's home, she walked slowly to her front door, turned to me and said, "I know I have to talk to Joey, but can you please give me an hour or so. I'm so very tired. Going to pick out April's dress and then going to the funeral home took a lot out of me."

"Of course, whatever you need. I got this."

When she went in to take her nap, I used the time to google all about children under five going to funerals, or participating in the viewing. I also googled what to say to them and how to say it. There was a wealth of information. What I focused on was what the professionals said and what individual people said about their own experience as a young child, or what their experience was with their own children.

It seemed clear from what I read that it was best to tell the child that their mother had died and would not be coming back. It was best to answer their questions, but not make up anything like the parent went to sleep, or went on a vacation. That would only confuse or frighten the child.

The information all made a lot of practical sense to me and with my psychology background, I knew it was the best course of action.

The information about viewing the body and going to funerals was a little more mixed. The best information I found was from a psychologist who had done a lot of work with children and funerals. He basically said no matter what age the child was, it was best to ask them if they'd like to go and see the parent. He said that he had never heard an adult who had been given a choice as a child, complain that they were angry or hurt by being given that choice.

Armed with this information, I went to relieve Franny of her babysitting duties. I figured that she'd need a break and that Joey might start getting concerned that she was left for such a long time.

I paused before my lemon tree in my backyard before heading up to my apartment. I dreaded what was to come and needed a moment to reflect.

I tried to focus on Joey and Aunt Carrie and how they needed support, but all I could think about was the murderer: Alex. As I stood before the tree, it occurred to me that if it wasn't Alex, then no one was safe anywhere. Just the thought that someone could strangle a beautiful young mother made me shudder at the cruelty of the world.

When I finally climbed the steps to my apartment and opened the door, all I could see was chaos. There was a tent made out of my sheets draped across my chairs. The floor was littered with hair bows and barrettes, coloring books and crayons, and an assortment of dishes that had food left over from what looked like peanut butter and jelly sandwiches.

Joey and Franny were hiding inside the tent. Well, not hiding, but I couldn't see them at first until I called out and they poked their heads out of the opening.

"Wow, it looks like you guys were having a lot of fun."

Franny gracefully exited from the tent and looked a bit chagrinned at the mess they had made.

"It's okay. The important things was that you guys were having a good time."

"Just give me a minute and I'll help you clean up."

"No need, Franny. Joey's grandma is taking a nap, but when she wakes up, Joey will have to go back to her house."

I then turned toward Joey and told her that her Nana and I had gone to her house and brought back some of her clothes and toys. I even brought back Lucy."

"You brought Lucy? Where is she? She must have been so scared without me. Let's go get her."

"Okay, Joey. She's waiting for you at Nana's house, but Nana's still sleeping. Can you help Franny and me clean up the floor here first? Then we'll go get Lucy."

Lucy was the cockeyed stuffed bear she had taken from my office months ago. Lucy came to her when her life was disorganized by her mother kicking her dad out of the house. There had been some turmoil and the bear in my office had spoken to her. Lucy was her comfort now.

I looked at Franny and asked her if she would like to come to the funeral home with us to see A-p-r-i-l.

"Do you want me to come, MJ?"

At first I thought I was just being polite in asking her since she spent the morning looking after Joey, but when she asked the question, I realized that I really did want her to come.

I felt that the more adults there were to handle the situation, the better. Especially if Joey needed to be taken somewhere where she felt safe, if she was going to be at the viewing.

"Franny, I think we need you to come. Someone has to be with Aunt Carrie, and someone has to tend to Joey."

"Then I'd be honored to come with you guys. Can I go like this?" She had on blue jeans and a halter top. Aunt Carrie and I had gone with slacks and blouses, so it seemed like Franny would pass except for the halter top. I opened my closet door and asked her to select a nice blouse. It was too hot to wear a suit jacket and it wasn't a funeral we were going to, but a viewing. No one was going to be there to judge. And besides, a young woman had been murdered. Who cared what it was we wore, except to show respect.

"Joey, can you start picking up the crayons while I help Franny select a nice blouse?"

Joey was happy to pick the crayons up and it kept her preoccupied while I took Franny to the side and in a low voice told her that we were going to be telling Joey that her mother was not coming back when Aunt Carrie woke up. I asked her if she could watch Joey in Joey's room while she looked over the toys and clothes we had brought back for her, so I could talk to Aunt Carrie about what I had learned about small children losing a parent.

"MJ, have they found Alex yet?"

"No, and I'm really hating him right now. First of all, if he didn't kill April, then where the heck is he? He's her father. He should be involved with this, right? If he isn't hiding from the police, then he has totally abdicated his responsibility as a parent. I want to strangle him."

Franny concurred and after she changed into a respectable blouse, all three of us made our way over to Aunt Carrie's house and into the kitchen.

Aunt Carrie was sitting at the table with milk and her famous chocolate chip cookies she kept frozen in her freezer for any occasion where they were needed.

Joey ran to her outstretched arms and Aunt Carrie scooped her up onto her lap. She poured her a glass of milk and offered Joey a cookie.

She gestured for us to sit and have some cookies and milk too, which we did. We were all trying to act as normal as possible for Joey. The time to tell her that her mother had died was getting closer and closer and I could feel my anxiety level going up.

After we all finished our cookies and milk, I suggested that Joey go look over her clothes and toys we had brought back, reminding her that Lucy was waiting for her in her room. I told her that Franny would go with her because Nana and I had to talk about something for a little while. Grown up, boring stuff.

Joey skipped to her room with Franny following close behind. I rapidly turned to Aunt Carrie and told her what I had learned from my research about how to tell a child their parent had died, and about letting the child make the decision if she wanted to go to the viewing or not.

"We can't put it off any longer, Aunt Carrie. She's going to feel things no matter when you tell her and she'll need her questions answered. I have faith that you'll be able to do it in the best way possible for Joey. And I'll be right here. I'm not going to leave you alone, if you'd like me to stay."

She dried her eyes and told me that she was ready. She wanted me to stay and Franny could hang out in the background. She felt she needed all of the support she could get.

Chapter 18

As we were about to get up from the kitchen table and go get Joey, Aunt Carrie's cell rang and she answered it immediately. It was Detective Myer returning her call about the young man April had befriended.

Aunt Carrie put her on speaker so I could hear what she had to say. I was hoping that this young man would be a good lead, but at the same time, I wanted it to be Alex. If it wasn't Alex, then he'd get to keep Joey and most likely would not allow Aunt Carrie to see her. And he'd for sure not allow me to see her since I had supported April leaving him. He probably hated me as much as I hated him.

Just as Aunt Carrie finished her call with the Detective, Joey came bounding into the kitchen with Lucy tucked under arm. "Look, Nana, Lucy's here."

Her pure joy was short-lived because her nana and I were sitting at the table with a look on our faces that showed that everything was not fine.

Joey caught us looking as we did before we were able to plaster the fake smiles on our faces. She stopped and looked between the two of us with a look of concern.

"Is this about Mommy?"

Kids have the ability to sense things that grown ups can't anymore. Joey knew something was wrong. She'd known it for a day and a half already, but everyone had been determined to deny there was anything wrong. She asked a direct question. It was time to answer.

I kept staring at Aunt Carrie, willing her to speak, but she sat frozen. I reached over and touched her hand and said, "Aunt Carrie, Joey wants to know what happened to her mommy."

"Nana?"

"Aunt Carrie, Joey's asking you something; can you answer her?"

Tears welled up in her eyes and she looked at Joey and motioned her to come sit on her lap.

Joey obliged, "What's wrong, Nana? You cwying?"

She could not stop her tears and when Joey reached up to touch them, she cried even harder as she tried to choke out the words, "MJ, I can't. . . I can't talk."

"It's okay, Aunt Carrie. It's okay," and I patted her arm, gave her a tissue, and then looked at Joey, my own tears glistening in my eyes.

"Joey, something really sad happened. Remember when you had to call the police and they came and broke into your house? Remember how brave you were by not unlocking the door, just as your mommy taught you?"

"Yes, my mommy told me to never open the door to stwangus."

"That's right. You were such a good girl. You didn't open the door to strangers and Mommy would have been very proud of you."

"Where is Mommy?"

"That's what your Nana and I want to tell you."

I took a deep breath and looked at Aunt Carrie to confirm if it was okay for me to tell Joey what happened. She shook her head yes.

"Well, something happened to your mommy and she died that night. That's why you were left alone in your house. She couldn't be with you because she wasn't able to come. She would have never left you alone if she could help it. Do you understand?"

"Yes, but whea is she?"

"Well, she can no longer walk or talk like we can. When someone dies, they aren't really here anymore. They can't breathe, they can't talk, they can't walk, they can't play with you, or read you bedtime stories anymore."

"Who will wead to me at night?"

"Well, for now, your nana will. She loves you very much, but she feels really sad that your mommy won't be coming to get you."

Joey sat there on her nana's lap and looked at me, then looked up at her nana's sad face. I didn't know if she understood anything I just said to her. She didn't cry or act upset, but looked puzzled.

"Joey, do you have any questions about what I just told you?"

Her little eyebrows knit together and her apparent puzzlement deepened as she asked, "Whea is she? Can I go see Mommy?"

It was more difficult than I imagined. Here I had been worried that she'd cry and carry on emotionally and instead she seemed calm and interested and was very much wanting to know if she could go see her mother.

Listening to our exchange finally got Aunt Carrie engaged. She blew her nose, turned Joey to face her and said, "Joey, your mother died. She's not coming back. You can't go to where she is. People who die can't be with us who are still alive. Remember when your goldfish died?"

"Yes."

"Well, it's like that. The fish didn't swim anymore, right? It just floated in the water because it wasn't alive anymore. That's what has happened to your mother, except she's not in water. She can't open her eyes, or talk to you, or hold you anymore. If she could talk, she'd tell you that she's so sorry that she died and will always love you, but she can't be with you anymore."

I think Joey finally started to understand. Not about death, but that her mother would not be coming to get her and she started to cry, saying, "I want my mommy. I want my mommy."

The three grown-ups in the room started crying with her. Franny and I formed a circle around Nana and Joey and hugged them, all of us feeling our own grief and the sadness and heartbreak of hearing a little girl cry for the mother who will never hold her again.

When all of our tears were spent for the moment, I suggested that maybe it would be okay to ask Joey if she'd like to go with us to see her mother, but first we'd have to explain exactly what she would be seeing.

Aunt Carrie took charge at this point and told Joey that we would all be going to see her mother later that day. She explained to her that her mother would look like she was sleeping and she'd look a bit different because she was no longer alive. She told her that Joey could talk to her, but her mother would not be able to answer her because she couldn't talk or walk anymore, as was already explained to her.

"You don't have to go, Joey. Franny could stay here with you again and you could play if you'd rather not go see your mommy."

"Could I make her a picture and give it to her?"

"Of course you can. Why don't you go get your paper and crayons in your room and you can draw her a picture here on the kitchen table until it's time to go."

We all looked on in amazement as Joey, Lucy Bear in hand, ran to her room to get her paper and crayons.

Children really were special. They were resilient, and they also were blessed with not fully understanding that death meant permanent. Children live in the moment and don't really understand what forever means. They seem to be spared some of the immediate pain that we as adults feel when someone close to us dies.

"Aunt Carrie, you did a really good job. We all did," I said when Joey was out of the room, "Let's see how it goes at the funeral home. If she becomes scared or wants to leave, either Franny or I can take her out for a walk, or to the car. Let's take the paper and crayons with us so she will have something to do if need be."

With that we all concurred. Joey came back with not only crayons, but watercolors and brushes and set about making her mommy a book.

"You're making Mommy a book?" I asked.

"Yes, Mommy likes books."

"What's the book going to be about?"

"Since Mommy won't be coming back and she can't talk to me, then I want her to have a book she can read and have the book to wememba me by."

Chapter 19

When we arrived at the funeral home, the same gentleman was waiting for us and ushered us into a waiting area where there was soft music playing. We all, including Joey, were mesmerized into stillness and none of us spoke.

Aunt Carrie had explained to Joey in more detail what it would be like to see her mother and what would be expected of her. She was told that she could leave her book with her mother and if she wanted to touch or kiss her mother, she could, but she didn't have to. Once again, she was reminded that her mother was dead and wouldn't be able to hold her, or play with her, or talk to her.

Death was such an odd concept for a child. I felt that it might actually be helpful for Joey to see her mother. I read in my research that it often helped children, and also adults, to view the dead body. It made it real to them. Otherwise, it would be difficult to understand what happened and there might be a constant hope that the deceased would somehow come back, or they'd get to see them again. That's why it was so important that soldiers who died in battle be brought back, so their loved ones could see them again and know for certain that they died. Never knowing for sure was a stress on family members.

Finding my own father dead was very traumatic to me, but I never for a moment doubted that he was dead. I was only left with questions about why he killed himself. There is a part of me that still thinks he didn't do it to himself; that he was murdered. But I also know that is a way of justifying why he'd choose to leave me behind. If he chose to end his life, it would mean that he didn't care about me. Except I know that people who commit suicide are usually in unbearable emotional pain. I did not want my father to suffer that kind of pain and maybe it was better that he killed himself, because he no longer had to endure that pain.

All these thoughts and feelings about my father came back to me as we drove to the mortuary. We had all been quiet; even Joey. I think the adults were all thinking the same thought. How would Joey handle seeing her dead mother?

It seemed to be taking a long time until they were ready to show us into the viewing room. We all seemed to huddle together and moved as one as we entered the room where we'd be able to see April one last time.

She was lying in a beautiful casket. I couldn't remember us looking at caskets. Did we? Or did they just pick one for the viewing? I had no idea how it all worked. I was sure that Aunt Carrie did not care how much it cost. She had more than enough money and I'm sure she wanted the best for April.

As we moved together toward April, I noticed that I was holding Joey's little hand. It was so small. She was so tiny. It was such a big event for such a small child. I realized that I was squeezing her hand too tight and mentally tried to loosen my grip.

When Aunt Carrie saw April, she lost it. She flung herself on top of April in the coffin and sobbed, telling her she was so sorry and that she loved her so much.

I looked down at Joey, expecting her to react in some way. Instead, she reached out her little arms and hugged her nana at the knees. Aunt Carrie turned and picked Joey up and hugged her to her chest, telling her that she loved her so much and that she was going to take care of her from now on.

Franny and I looked at each other. I saw that Franny had a horrified look on her face so I quickly went up to Joey and Aunt Carrie and hugged them both. I then took Joey from her grandmother's arms and showed her April lying in the coffin. She was dressed in her beautiful purple dress with her multicolored quilt spread in a way that covered her lower body. She looked peaceful. They had done a good job with make-up, but she didn't look like she did when she was alive.

"Joey, do you want to give your mother your book?"

Joey clung to me and just looked at her mother, her eyes wide.

"It's okay, Joey. You don't have to if you don't want to. You can keep your book and read it out loud whenever you miss your mommy. Would you like to go now?"

Joey stared at her mother without answering me. She finally said, "She doesn't look wight."

"That's right, Joey. Your mommy isn't really here with us anymore. Remember we told you that she can't talk to us or move. Her life force is no longer in her body, but you can still talk to her if you'd like."

Joey then looked me in the eyes and said, "I want to go back to Nana's house."

"Okay, let's go wait out in the car for your nana."

I carried her outside and put her down to walk to the car. She held my hand, but kept looking back at the funeral home.

"Joey, how about we just sit here on this bench for a bit. Do you have any questions for me?"

She was extraordinarily quiet. I started to worry that it was the wrong thing to do, to bring her to see her mother. I tried not to feel anxious and made myself relax my muscles which had tensed up when Aunt Carrie lost it.

I knew Aunt Carrie needed to be alone with April. She wanted to tell her all the things she never had a chance to tell her. I could only imagine how painful it was for her, but also how very important it was for her to have this time alone with April.

Joey was leaning in to me, so I asked her if she'd like to sit on my lap, and she nodded her head yes.

We sat together as the sun started to set. The warm air felt good and I could almost imagine that it was a beautiful day sitting together with this wonderful child nestled into my arms, instead of a trauma for her. I vowed then and there that I'd be present for her, since hopefully, she'd be living right next door to me. I would try my best to show her she was loved and I knew Aunt Carrie would too.

After a while, I asked Joey if she'd like to read the book she made to me. It was one sheet of paper folded in a way to show 4 pages of her colorful drawings and watercoloring. I noticed that there was scribbling, in what I assumed were the words that Joey had wanted to write.

She pulled away from me and opened her book and began to read, "Mommy, I love you. I miss you. I wish you could come and pick me up. I love Nana, but I want to live with you, but I know I can't. Love Joey."

"Joey, that is a very nice book and I love all the colors you used. Your mommy would be so proud of you."

Just then I saw an elderly couple come up the walk. They were dressed all in black and looked rather austere. The woman was stick thin and taller than the man, who had a bit of a paunch and wore an expensive suit. He was looking down as the woman walked with purpose, head held high, up to the funeral home.

As they got closer to where we were sitting, the woman stopped in front of us and said, "Is this Joey?"

She had on an expensive fashionable black dress and a black hat with a black veil hiding her face. She looked like she just stepped out of a movie as a wealthy aristocrat going to a funeral. She held herself with self-confidence and entitlement.

Joey recoiled from them and curled her little body closer to mine.

I didn't know these people, so did not want to admit who Joey was until I understood who they were. "And you are?"

"I'm Estelle Spark, and this is my husband Benjamin Spark."

Benjamin reached over to shake my hand, which I shook with a bit of hesitation. However, the woman did not offer hers, but said instead, "We are Joey's grandparents. Such a tragedy losing her mother. And since her father is next of kin, we've come to ensure she has a good home and stellar education."

Chapter 20

All I could do was stare at them. They were Alex's parents? I honestly didn't even know he had parents who were still alive. I had never heard about them from either April or Aunt Carrie. Was she implying that they were going to take Joey to live with them? I also wondered how they even knew about the viewing.

The fact that they had to ask if the child I held on my lap was even Joey spoke volumes. Obviously they had had nothing to do with Joey in the past and the obvious question was: where the hell was Alex. Why wasn't Alex here instead of them?

I held Joey tight against me. No way in hell would I let those two take my precious Joey. It would kill Aunt Carrie. I looked around to see if Aunt Carrie was anywhere around. There was no sign of her, nor of Franny. I assumed Franny had stayed with Aunt Carrie in case she needed any help.

I had an immediate aversion toward Estelle and it seemed as if Joey did also. Even though it was none of my business, I blurted out, "You will not be taking Joey with you, and by the way, where is Joey's father?"

My voice most likely sounded aggressive and it didn't seem to phase Estelle one bit. She just smiled in a condescending way, or maybe it was more of a smirk. I couldn't really tell because her black veil hid her face.

"My dear," her voice sounded strident to me and I couldn't help but grimace. "I don't know who you are, but I'm assuming you're Joey's nanny, so would you please direct me to Carrie Pedersen?"

The nerve of that woman. Assuming I was Joey's nanny. No way was I going to help her out. Let her figure out where Carrie Pedersen was herself. It was confusing. How could this woman, who claimed to be Joey's grandmother, come waltzing into her life out of nowhere, and not even recognize her own grandchild? It was obvious to me that they had never bothered to see her or have any contact with her. And I wondered why I hadn't ever heard of them.

Joey was burrowed into me like a scared puppy. No way did she know these people. Or, if she did, she was scared of them. They scared me too. To be honest, Benjamin didn't scare me, but Estelle was downright frightening. She reminded me of a wicked witch, all dressed in black with that black veil covering up her face like a mask.

At that moment, I saw Franny lead Aunt Carrie out the funeral home door and help her down the steps. The colorful quilt was clutched in her hands and she was leaning on Franny like an old woman. She seemed to have aged ten years from the time she entered the mortuary to the time she left.

I could hardly bear the thought that she'd have to face Joey's other grandparents who were standing in front of me. She had enough to deal with as it was with the loss of her daughter. I just knew it wasn't going to be a good encounter, but felt powerless to stop it.

I sat there clutching Joey to me and watched as Aunt Carrie looked up and saw the Sparks standing in front of Joey. It surprised me when they seemed to know each other, because Aunt Carrie let go of Franny's arm and walked toward them and held out her hand to shake first Estelle's, and then Benjamin's hand.

I couldn't figure out what was going on and tried to catch Aunt Carrie's eye. Franny just stood still at the bottom of the steps where Aunt Carrie had left her, just as confused as I was.

After a moment of silence amongst all of us, Aunt Carrie turned to me and asked me if I could take Joey on a walk in order to give them some privacy, but Estelle said, "We can talk later; Benji and I want to go view the body."

Looking at their elegant attire and the Rolex watch Benjamin sported, one could tell they were wealthy and assumed they could do whatever they wished without having to consider other people.

And she was correct. There was no discussion and she started toward the funeral home. When she noticed her husband wasn't following her, she turned to him with a glare and made a small motion with her hand for him to follow. He had the decency to look at us apologetically before taking off after her.

Clearly, we knew who wore the pants in that household, and I wondered where all the money came from. It didn't seem like Benjamin had the balls to make the kinds of decisions necessary for someone who made that kind of money. No, I'm sure the wealth came from Estelle's family and I'm sure she used it to get what she wanted.

But why would she want Joey, if that really was what she was after?

I turned to Aunt Carrie who saw the questioning look on my face and before I could speak she said, "MJ, don't, not now, not in front of Joey."

I looked over at Franny and called her over. "Franny, can you and Joey go look at that beautiful fountain over there for a minute?"

As Franny started to take Joey from me, Joey grabbed for her grandmother and started crying. Aunt Carrie took her into her arms and gave her a big hug and told her that she had to talk to me for a moment. Then she told her that we'd be able to go soon and maybe even stop for an ice cream on the way home if she was a good girl and went with Franny for a bit.

After Franny and Joey left to walk over to the fountain, I turned to Aunt Carrie and exploded with all the questions I had. "Where did those people come from and how do you know them? You've met them before, right? Why are they here? How dare they come to April's viewing without being invited. Especially when their son killed her. How did they even know there was a viewing today?"

"I told them."

"What?"

"I told them, MJ. I met them years ago when I first came out to California when April first got pregnant. It's a long story.

I honestly thought they weren't in the picture anymore, but apparently they are."

"Why did you invite them to the viewing?" To me, they seemed like awful people. "They said they were here to ensure Joey had a good home. Does that mean they want to take her? Tell me that's not true."

I was horrified to think that strangers could just come and take Joey with them, even if they were her grandparents. My gut told me that Estelle and Benjamin were up to no good. And I wanted an answer: Where was their son?

Aunt Carrie sat down heavily on the bench and said, "No, they can't take Joey with them without some kind of court order. I'm sure they have their lawyers working on some legal way they can take her. MJ, they heard about April's murder and the disappearance of their son and called me. It was Benjamin who talked to me. He sounded sympathetic and concerned and wanted to know if there was anything they could do for me. I thanked him and told him I had support and it was all handled."

"Okay, so why are they here?"

Aunt Carrie had just said good-bye to her only child; we shouldn't even have been talking about who was going to be taking Joey. Aunt Carrie shouldn't have had to deal with those people and I felt a little ashamed that I was pressing her for information.

"As I said, I invited them. Well, I didn't really invite them, but I told Benjamin what funeral home I was using. I guess they must have called to find out the details." She let out a long sigh. "They're going to be a problem. They have a lot of money and are used to having their way. Estelle doesn't want Joey in order to love her and give her a beautiful life. She wants Joey because she thinks she owns her, just like she thought she owned Alex, until he disappointed her so badly that she disowned him."

"I see. So they probably don't know where Alex is, right?"

"I doubt it. They washed their hands of him a long time ago. The only thing Estelle is interested in is the fact that Joey has Spark DNA. It means everything to her. Joey is part of their bloodline. That's why they came to see April when she got pregnant."

"But they haven't been in touch since Joey was born, right?"

"Well, if they had wanted to be involved, they'd have had to be involved with their son, Alex, and they didn't want anything to do with him."

I got it. April was dead and Alex disappeared. It was a perfect time for them, or actually Estelle, to swoop in and get their granddaughter, the only heir to all of that fortune, I assumed. I guessed their plan was to take Joey and have her raised by nannies after which they'd send her off to some exclusive boarding school where she'd learn how to be a rich heiress. It would be such a cruel fate for Joey, and so cold.

"Aunt Carrie, you can't let them take Joey. You have to get a lawyer now. I'm sorry you can't grieve properly, but this can't wait. I get a really bad feeling about these people. They probably already have papers showing they are the legal guardians. Did April have a will? Did she arrange for you to be Joey's legal guardian if something happened to her?"

After seeing the look on her face, I knew April hadn't done that. Aunt Carrie stood up, looking defeated. When she started to sway on her feet, Franny noticed and ran over with

Joey following, and together we helped Aunt Carrie sit back down on the bench.

After informing Franny what was going on, Franny, being one of the richest people I knew, immediately read the situation and offered her help. She had good family lawyers herself, and took out her phone to make a call. It was evening, but I'm sure she had some kind of direct line to lawyers, any time day or night. She didn't even ask for permission, but I heard her talk into the phone requesting someone come to Aunt Carrie's address within the next couple of hours.

At that moment, I was grateful that I had a friend like Franny. As much as she was a bit self-centered, she was always available to help out her good friends in need. No questions asked. I looked at her and mouthed a 'thank you.'

Joey stood looking up at us, her homemade book clutched to her chest. I smiled down at her and asked if she was ready to go get some ice cream. She grinned up at me and said, "Can I have bubblegum ice cweam, in a cone?"

"Anything you want, Sweetheart."

She then looked pensive and said, "Can I go see Mommy again? I want to give her my book."

"Of course you can, would you like Nana to come with you?" I looked anxiously at Aunt Carrie to see if she could tolerate going back into the funeral home.

"Could you come with me, MJ? I want to give Mommy a kiss and I don't think Nana can lift me up that high."

I didn't relish seeing Estelle and Benjamin again, but I couldn't deny Joey, so I agreed to go with her.

We passed Joey's other grandparents on our way to see April again. Estelle didn't even acknowledge us, but Benjamin nodded his head to me as we passed.

When we were beside April's coffin, I lifted Joey up so she could lay her book onto her mother's chest.

She then reached her little hand out and tentatively touched her mother's face, but withdrew it quickly saying, "She cold."

"Yes, she is."

"I don't want to give her a kiss."

"You don't have to, but would you like to blow her a kiss?"

Her face lit up at the suggestion and she kissed her hand and blew it toward her mother. I broke down in tears and Joey looked at me with concern.

"I'm okay, Joey. It's okay to be sad when someone dies. You might feel sad too in the days to come. You can cry for your mommy. You can tell us when you're sad. It's okay."

I put her down and we walked out hand in hand. I wished I could do more for this precious child. I especially wished I could keep Alex and his parents away from her.

Chapter 21

Holding her little hand as we left the funeral home made me feel extra protective of her. She was so small. I wanted to take her to live with me and never let her out of my sight. Never had I been so aware of how vulnerable children are when placed in our care. We are their guardians and need to protect them and make sure they were taken care of and loved. I intended to do just that. Along with Aunt Carrie, of course.

I saw that the grandparents had already left and I asked Franny and Aunt Carrie if everything was all right. They mumbled something that I didn't hear. I can't really hear when people mumble, or speak softly, or I can't read their lips. It was just something I put up with having a 50% hearing loss, but at times it was annoying, so I repeated, "Is everything all right?"

Franny assured me that things were going to be all right just as soon as her lawyers got involved. Aunt Carrie just sat and kept wiping her eyes. The quilt was on her lap, but she didn't take it off, even though the weather was still very warm.

Joey hadn't forgotten that we had promised her ice cream, so we stopped at an ice cream place and got her two scopes of some type of rainbow colored ice cream. The rest of us were too wound up to eat anything.

Delighting in having her ice cream cone, Joey licked it as we continued to Aunt Carrie's house. Franny fretted about stopping to get the ice cream because she didn't want to keep her lawyer waiting. Apparently, he was doing her a favor by coming out to the house, and in the evening at that.

Franny has a lot of pull, but she hesitates to use it. She felt this was an important occasion but didn't want to take advantage of her lawyer.

We beat the lawyer to Aunt Carrie's house and I took Joey up to my apartment while they discussed the legalities of child custody when parents were both absent. I thought that Franny would be a better person to help Aunt Carrie with child custody than I would be because she has had to deal with a lot of legal issues in her lifetime. I was happy to get the information later.

Joey and I climbed the stairs to my apartment. There was someone waiting for me at the top of the stairs, but in my emotional state, it didn't even register until they spoke.

"MJ, it's me."

Jesse.

I stopped short but Joey kept climbing the stairs, eager to get into my apartment to play with all the great things Franny had brought over earlier. Her hands were sticky from her ice cream cone and now mine was too. I wiped my hand on my slacks as I retrieved my keys.

Jesse was dressed in his police uniform and Joey didn't hesitate for a minute as she walked up to my door and, turning to me demanded, "Huwwee up, MJ."

Jesse knelt down to her level and asked her where the fire was, but Joey didn't understand and said, "No fia."

He laughed and patted her head as he stood, looking down at me.

"What are you doing here, Jesse?"

"I was in the neighborhood and thought I'd stop a minute to see if there was anything I could do for you guys. I see that you've got the little one under control. How's your Aunt Carrie?"

"You remember that she's not really my aunt, right?"

"Of course I remember. How is she doing?"

I was so happy to see him, but at the same time, worried that I was going to fall for his kindness and start having hope that we could somehow be together. I kept my tone light and said, "We just got back from viewing April. Aunt Carrie's with Franny now and about to talk to one of Franny's hot shot lawyers."

"Why is she talking to a lawyer?"

As I started to explain about the other grandparents, Joey became agitated and said, "MJ, I need to go to the bathwoom."

"I'm so sorry, Joey. Here let me get the door."

No sooner had I gotten it opened, when Joey ran in and started taking all the precious gifts Franny had brought out of their bags. The items we had so carefully returned to the bags earlier.

"I thought you had to go to the bathroom."

"I punked you."

I ruffed her hair and smiled at her. I doubted she really knew what 'punked' meant.

I turned to Jesse, who had already stepped into my apartment, but asked anyway, "Would you like to come in?"

"You were about to explain something to me out on the landing?"

I invited him to sit down and as Joey took her precious items out of the bags and started playing with them, I told Jesse in hushed tones all about the grandparents showing up at the funeral home and how they threatened to take Joey. They can't do that, I don't think, can they? April didn't leave a will stating who she wanted as Joey's legal guardian. I hadn't heard a word about the Sparks until today. I guess they have a lot of money and influence and think they can manipulate the system into giving them their grandchild. I'm so worried.

Sharing my fears with Jesse made me realize just how close I had gotten to Joey. I also knew that Estelle didn't actually say she was going to take Joey, but that she wanted to ensure Joey had a good home and education. Maybe all she wanted to do was give Joey all that money could buy. "She had on this hat with a black veil hiding her face, but her essence felt like a Cruella de Vil."

He laughed at the image of Cruella but then immediately got serious and tried to reassure me. I was eager to hear what the lawyer said, but knew it would be a while before I heard anything.

My stomach growled so loud, Jesse and Joey both heard it and laughed. I hadn't eaten since the early morning when Aunt Carrie had made us breakfast and then realized that Joey had eaten nothing for dinner except her ice cream.

"I'm hungry. Who wants to eat?"

"Let me go grab us a pizza," Jesse said, "I'm hungry too and I know the best pizza this side of town. Pepperoni?"

"Yeah, peppewoni, but no olives and no onions and no bwoccoli."

"A girl after my own heart," Jesse said and leaned down to tweak Joey's nose.

Jesse seemed good with kids. His kids were lucky to have him as a dad.

A yearning thought popped into my head as I imagined Jesse, Joey, and me as a family. I shook my head to clear that vision because I knew it was never going to happen. Jesse was still married, and Joey wasn't mine. But the yearning for a family of my own was still there. It made me sad to think that I was never going to have that family. I thought I had made my peace with this reality, but seeing Jesse and Joey together in my place stirred it all up again.

As Jessed opened the door to go get our pizza, he stopped and asked if we wanted soda pop too.

Soda pop. Who called it soda pop? I laughed and asked Joey if she was allowed to drink soda.

"Sometimes my mommy lets me drink orange soda as a special tweat. Is it a special tweat?"

"Yes, yes it is," I said.

"You got it, Joey. And what can I get for you, MJ?"

"Coke or Pepsi would hit the spot."

"Okay, orange soda pop and a Pepsi it is."

He turned to leave but turned back when I called out his name, "Jesse,"

"Yeah?"

"Thanks."

"Sure, no problem."

Chapter 22

It was late by the time we had finished all but two pieces of the giant pizza Jesse had brought back. Now I could feel the trauma of the day take over.

Joey climbed up onto Jesse's lap and promptly fell asleep. I felt my eyelids close as I sat on my therapy chair across from them. I hadn't noticed I'd fallen asleep until I felt my cell phone vibrate in my pocket.

I jumped up, instantly alert, and dug into my pocket to retrieve my phone. It was Franny.

"Hi, Franny, are you guys finished?"

"We are. Finally. Aunt Carrie was bone-tired so I sent her to bed. I told her that you and I would take care of Joey and for her not to worry. Can I come over?"

"Yes, I'm dying to know what the lawyer said."

"Okay, I'm on my way."

"Franny?"

"Yes?"

"Jesse's here."

There was silence for a few minutes and then she said, "Okay. Thanks for the heads up."

Franny was not a big fan of Jesse since he decided to go back to his wife, who had kicked him out and was living with another man at the time, and had actually started divorce procedures. But then his wife had asked him to try again, for the kids. I think she was still in love with him, but couldn't handle the hours and the fears of living with a cop.

Franny eyed the leftover pizza and when I indicated for her to help herself, she grabbed a piece and practically inhaled it without taking a breath.

"I love this pizza. It's the best pizza. Beats anything you could get in New York, and that's saying a lot."

Jesse looked over at me and said, "See, what did I tell you. The best this side of the freeway."

I was glad that Franny and Jesse could bond over knowing where one could find the best pizza. It broke the tension between them and I could relax, knowing I didn't have to referee them. If nothing else, Franny was very protective of me.

"I'm dying to hear what your lawyer said about Joey's custody. Joey's sound asleep and didn't even move when you came in and started talking. You don't think she'll hear what we are saying do you?"

Jesse picked up one of Joey's little arms and dropped it. It fell like lead and Joey didn't make a peep. This act made me feel secure that Joey was in a deep sleep so I indicated for Franny to tell us what happened.

"Well, first he gave us information on what happens if both parents die without wills. Of course, we don't know if Alex is alive or dead and we don't know if he had a will or not. But if both parents have died without a will, then it goes to the courts and the court decides what's best for the child. They usually pick the person that is the closest to the child and they always put the best interest of the child above anything else.

"So in this case, Carrie Pedersen, her maternal grandmother, would be the best choice since she's been so involved with Joey. Since the Sparks haven't been involved with Joey as far as we know, Joey would not go to them. However, anyone can contest that decision and the Sparks probably will. They'll say they have the means to make Joey's life extraordinarily great, so she should be given that chance."

I put my hand to my chest and shook my head back and forth, willing the last bit of information to go away.

"The good news," Franny continued, "is that as I first stated, the courts always put the child's needs first. So it's not always about money. If the child has a close connection to a close family member or a close friend, then they think of that as being the best for the child."

I hadn't realized I was holding my breath and I let it out in a sigh of relief when I heard that.

"So most likely, Joey will go to her nana, Aunt Carrie, right?" I asked.

"Most likely, unless the other grandparents come up with some other compelling reason why they should have her. Plus, Alex is still missing, so if Alex shows up and he's cleared of the murder, then Alex gets her."

I may go to hell for having this thought, but I prayed that Alex stayed gone. I didn't wish him dead, but I did not want him found, unless they could prove he murdered April. After all he was the most likely suspect.

Jesse wasn't on the case, but he was able to get information about how the investigation was going. He told us that there was no real evidence against Alex, which was a mystery to me. He must have planned it ahead of time and worn gloves and some kind of body suit that didn't leave any trace of himself. Otherwise, if it wasn't him and it was a crime of convenience, there would have been some evidence that someone else had been there that night and there wasn't any.

He did say that the detectives had looked into the kid Aunt Carrie told them about. He was the teenager in the neighborhood that April had befriended. He had shared with her how he had been bullied in his younger years and April had been trying to help him. His mother reported that the kid was on the autistic spectrum and vouched for him, saying he was at home that night, asleep in bed.

My head was spinning and I was exhausted. I needed to go to sleep. There was nothing we could do, at that moment anyway.

After finishing the last piece of pizza, Franny grabbed one of the sodas and drank deeply, giving out a huge belch when finished.

Jesse looked surprised since it was such an incongruous thing to see this beautiful, elegant creature do such a tactless thing. It took him by surprise and his face showed it.

Franny grinned her mischievous grin and laughed.

"I'm impressed, Ms. Franny. I don't think I could compete with anything near that belch. I'm surprised it didn't wake Joey."

It felt good to me that they were sparring. One less thing for me to worry about. When Franny stood and took her leave, I got up and walked her to the door, gave her a big hug and thanked her profusely. After she left, I kept standing at the door expecting Jesse to leave also, but he didn't move from the sofa, leaving Joey's blond, curly head on his lap.

"Jesse, you have to go."

"Why?"

"You know why. Besides, there's no place for you to sleep here. Joey and I will be sleeping on the sofa bed. I don't have any other place for you to sleep."

"I just want to stay here and protect you."

"From what?"

"I don't really know. Call it cop's instinct. Something doesn't smell right about this whole case and you know I worry about you, and now I worry about Joey, too."

Chapter 23

His words startled me. "What do you mean?"

"Think about it, MJ. There is not a trace of Alex anywhere. He hasn't used his credit cards. His car is still at his place. None of his friends nor anyone at his work has heard from him. There is no hint that he flew out of here. It's like he just disappeared. Poof!"

Jesse was telling me things that I had not heard from the investigation, so upon a moment of reflection, I had to agree with him. It was very strange.

"Okay, let's say he planned the murder and had a lot of cash stashed away somewhere and another car he could drive away with. Maybe he even had false ID's made for himself. That's possible, right?"

"Yes," Jesse drew the word out as he was prone to do.

"But what?"

"I think it's highly improbable."

"Why? He was angry at April. He hated her for leaving him. Guys like that don't like losing what they think of as theirs. You know, it's just like his wicked mother. She wants Joey because she thinks she owns her." I was getting heated and my voice grew louder.

Jesse looked down at the sleeping Joey and then made a hushing movement with his hands.

I sat and put my head in my hands. What was Jesse saying? It was too much of a coincidence that Alex disappeared the minute April was murdered. It had to be him.

"You didn't answer my question. Why is it not probable that Alex murdered her and then slipped away and went into hiding?"

"Well, for one, he had just won what he had wanted in terms of custody of Joey. He battled with April in the courts in order to hurt her by winning his right to keep Joey half-time. He would have relished torturing her even more by putting Joey in the middle. Killing her would have taken away all of his fun."

"You're right. He is a manipulating monster. He would have wanted the game he was playing with April to continue. But if he didn't kill her, who did? And why would he disappear right after her murder? It makes no sense."

"I know. That's why I'd like to stay here to protect both you and Joey. The fact that Joey's other grandparents showed up at this time seems relevant in some way. I just haven't figured out how they're involved, but trust me, they're involved."

"Do you think they helped Alex get away? Maybe they have a private jet. Is there any way to check that out? They have money. They could make him disappear."

"That's one possibility, but you told me they hadn't been talking for years. That Joey didn't even recognize them when they showed up today. Besides they had disowned Alex, right? Why would they all at once save him and help him disappear?"

"Maybe they see this as an opportunity. They wouldn't want a scandal that would surely happen if Alex were arrested for murder. They could disappear him and then get what they've always wanted. Control over Joey."

"Okay, I could see that happening. But they'd want to make sure he stayed disappeared."

I sat there looking at Jesse as I slowly understood what he might be saying. "You think they killed Jesse?"

"I don't think they killed him, no. They wouldn't get their hands dirty with murder, but they have money and connections to make sure he would never be a problem for them."

"So what you are implying is they killed April and did it in such a way that would frame Alex. Then got him out of the country but if he ever came back, he'd get charged with April's murder. That would ensure that he'd stay away. Like a blackmail scheme." I was thinking out loud and just the thought of April being murdered as a way to gain access to Joey just didn't make that much sense. There had to be more to it.

"So what do we do? Do you think the detectives who are on this case have a clue of what we've just been talking about?"

"I think they are as stumped as we are. Without any hard evidence, there's not much they can do."

I felt so defeated. My AA sponsor would tell me to leave it alone. Let it go. It wasn't my job. But looking across at the innocent little girl cuddled up on the sofa, I knew I couldn't let it go. I had to find out who killed her mother. I had to. Especially if Estelle had anything to do with it. I knew I couldn't allow even the threat of Joey going to live with her.

I suspected Estelle was in the middle of all of this, but didn't know how. The fact that she just showed up and started making comments about Joey made me feel very uncomfortable. I had to somehow come up with a plan. I needed to get Estelle to confess her part in all of this. But how?

Sometimes when I'd had a problem I couldn't solve, I'd sleep on it and the answer would come to me.

I told Jesse he had to leave and when he resisted I asked, "What are you going to do, live here? They're not going to kill Aunt Carrie or me. They'll be able to use their high-priced lawyers to take her from us legally. They aren't that stupid. If they were involved with April's murder, they have probably gotten away with it and they know it. They aren't going to take any more chances. Besides, I'm so tired, I need to sleep. This little one is going to be awake early in the morning and I need to be able to be awake to care for her. It may be a difficult day for her and she may be filled with questions about what she experienced today."

Seeing the wisdom in my speech, Jesse gently put Joey's head down on the sofa and quietly stood up and moved toward the door, "I hope you're right. I don't like it, but you're right, I can't stay with you guys around the clock. I'll drive by here frequently and ask my friends to keep an eye out for you."

His concern and asking his fellow cops to keep an eye out made me feel more secure. Watching him with Joey made my heart ache for a family with a husband who was that kind and gentle to his kids. Again, I mourned the fact that Gideon and I never got a chance to have children. I felt the sting of my forty-two years, knowing I was most likely too old to be able to get pregnant and that I had lost my chance of ever becoming a mother.

As he was going out the door, I stopped him and asked, "It's none of my business, but how is your wife dealing with you going back to active duty?"

He looked into my eyes and said, "How do you think?"

Yeah, he should have never gone back to her. He had made the wrong decision. And now it was too late.

But as I closed the door behind him, I wondered; *Is it really too late?*

Chapter 24

I had been right. Joey woke at the first light of day and sat up beside me on the sofa. I hadn't made the sofa into a bed because frankly I was too tired and I also didn't want to wake Joey in the middle of the night. I didn't get much sleep because I didn't want to move her, so I had to curl my larger body into the corner at the opposite side of the sofa.

"Hey, little one, good morning."

"I slept here?"

"Yes, you did. You conked out right after finishing your pizza. See, you're still in your clothes, and you didn't even brush your teeth."

She looked around, her hair a tangled mess and there were lines on her face from the blanket that was on the sofa. She looked darling and I wanted to grab and hug her, but also wanted to be mindful of how she might be feeling.

"Are you hungry, little one?"

"I'm not little. I'm a big gul."

"Of course you're a big girl. I called you little one because you are smaller than me. You don't want me to call you little one?"

She sat slumped against the back of the sofa to think about it, then said, "It's okay, I guess."

"Want me to fix you some breakfast?"

I looked at the clock. It was almost six o'clock. I imagined Aunt Carrie would be awake and most likely was cooking breakfast for us. So instead of trying to find something to make for breakfast, I suggested we go see if her nana was awake yet.

"Want to go see Nana? She probably misses you. She didn't get to kiss you good night last night and she didn't get to make you wash your face and brush your teeth."

Joey wrinkled her nose at the suggestion of brushing her teeth, so I sat up, grabbed her, and gave her a tickle. She screamed with giggles until I stopped and my face grew serious as I suggested I throw her in the tub because her feet smelled.

This brought on another squeal of laughter which prompted me to get up. I hadn't changed clothes either and smelled under my arms and wrinkled my nose and said with effect, "Yew."

I wasn't sure if I'd have time to take a quick shower, so I went into my little bathroom, stripped off my wrinkled clothes and washed my face and under my arms. I drew the towel around me and went into the living room to pull on a pair of shorts and t-shirt since I knew it was going to be another hot day.

"Your turn, Joey."

She got up from the sofa and slowly walked into the bathroom, yawning, forgetting to close the door.

When she was finished, I was ready to go and we made our way across my backyard to Aunt Carrie's house. I noticed that the workers had cleaned up a lot of the construction debris and I felt guilty for my total lack of attention to what was happening in the completion of my house. I made a mental note to do a walk-through soon and to look at all of my texts to see if I had gotten one from my contractor. I had been so consumed with April's murder and taking care of Joey that I had completely abdicated any responsibility for the finishing of my house.

I had gotten so used to living in my little office space up above my garage that I hadn't been giving the restoration of my old house any attention. But I knew it wasn't just April's murder. I still felt some anxiety whenever I went into the new house and remembered the night it burned down. Part of me wondered if it was even a good idea to rebuild and live in it again. I didn't have as many flashbacks as I had in the beginning, but I still had some nightmares about that night when I killed Mike Rimichi.

As we entered the back door to Aunt Carrie's, I thought it was imperative that she lock it with a deadbolt from now on until April's murder was figured out. Jesse had put fear into me with his musings about what actually happened to April and I had to admit he wasn't wrong.

Joey let go of my hand and went running into the kitchen where her beloved nana was making chocolate chip pancakes for us.

"I'm hungwe, Nana."

Nana gave Joey a big hug and told her to comb her hair, wash her hands, and then sit herself down.

Oops, I realized that is what I should have done with Joey. Maybe I wouldn't have been such a great mom after all. I didn't even know enough to comb Joey's hair or to make her wash her hands before sitting down for breakfast.

"MJ, pour yourself some coffee and sit. You'll eat with us, no?"

"Absolutely, I love your chocolate chip pancakes. And we have a lot to discuss."

"I know. I hired the lawyer Franny brought over last night. I decided that I needed to be proactive on this whole thing. There is no way I'll let Joey be taken from me by those uptight people."

"Uptight? That's what you're calling them?"

"I'm being polite and you know it."

I knew Aunt Carrie. She was one of the kindest people I knew. I also knew that if she were up against the wall, she would fight back like a tiger. I let out a sigh, knowing that it wasn't my battle, but I'd do everything in my power in order to make sure Joey stayed with her nana. Selfishly, it would also mean that Joey would be near me.

After we ate the pancakes and I drank my second cup of her bitter coffee, Joey asked if she could go to her room to play. We let her go without asking her to take a bath and change into new clothes. There was enough time for that later.

"I called April's school and informed them of the memorial I'm having at my house on Sunday. Can you be sure and let Franny know for me, and ask Jesse to come too? I'd like to pick his brain afterwards, if he's still willing to talk to me."

"I know he is, Aunt Carrie. He came over last night and we had a chance to talk about the investigation. There's things that just don't add up."

After explaining what Jesse and I had started to wonder about, Aunt Carrie became very quiet.

"I've upset you."

"No more than I already am, MJ. I'm just more determined than ever to protect Joey from Estelle and Benjamin."

"Aunt Carrie, I think it would be a good idea if I went to a meeting this morning. Are you going to be all right?"

"Of course, MJ. What was I thinking, taking up all of your time? You have a life and you need those meetings. You go. Joey and I will be just fine. We'll go shopping for some pretty flowers or something pretty for April's memorial."

"I love you and I'm so sorry you have to be going through this. It's just not fair."

"I've lived a long life so far, MJ, and I've learned that life is never fair. All we can do is react the best way we know how."

I felt there was something more to her life that she hadn't ever shared with me, but it didn't seem appropriate to talk about it just then.

"What time?"

"What time?"

"Yes, what time on Sunday should we come? And, can I help you with the food and drinks?"

"I'm actually going to have someone cater it. If it weren't April's memorial, it would be the one thing I'm good at doing—the food and drinks. But I just don't feel up to doing that much. I have no idea how many people will be here, but a neighbor of April's got hold of me and I guess the neighbors really liked her, so some of them will be coming too. I'm ordering enough for about twenty people."

"No one is coming to eat and drink. They're coming to be with you in your sorrow and to share stories about April. They're coming to laugh and cry with you."

I watched as she started to cry again. I knew it was going to take time for her to grieve. I imagined one may never get over losing a daughter, especially in such a cruel and unnecessary way. But it will get less painful as time goes on. I'm glad she has Joey to focus on.

I went to leave, but then turned back and asked again, "Time?"

Chapter 25

I went directly to my AA meeting and was greeted by many of the regulars. They had all been there when I broke down after first hearing about April. I smiled awkwardly at them and felt the hot flush creeping up my neck whenever I'm feeling ashamed or embarrassed, which is every time I'm the focus of attention.

I knew I should probably share about how I was feeling about April, but it felt so personal. I didn't want her to become the center focus for strangers to hang their triggered emotions on, so I kept quiet and was glad when the meeting was over.

It was weird, but Big Al wasn't at the meeting. I don't think I had ever been at that meeting without him there. I got in my car determined to use the morning to take care of my business, my house, and any other thing that I had neglected in the past several days. I punched in Big Al's number and listened to his voicemail, after which I left the message. "Hey, I noticed you weren't at the meeting this morning. Are you okay? I don't think I've ever been to the meeting when you weren't around. Please call, or text to reassure me that you are okay."

After I disconnected, I had an afterthought and texted him, "It's been a weird and painful couple of days being with Aunt Carrie and little Joey. We went to view April yesterday and Joey's other grandparents came and made a scene. I'll tell you all about it when we next talk. Let me know that you're okay. Seriously, I care about you."

Next, I called my contractor to see exactly when he was coming back from his cabin trip. His business partner answered and told me that he was actually at my house this morning, going over some of the last details. I thanked his partner and hurried home. I wanted to catch him before he left. It was just like him to come when I'm not there.

Finally, I tried to remember if I had any clients scheduled. I'm old fashioned in that I keep a paper calendar. I hate the smartphone calendars. The screen is too small. I need to see the entire 7 days in big letters. The problem is that I don't carry my paper calendar around with me, although I probably should. Now, I had to wait until I got back to my office.

After checking my client calendar, I saw that I didn't have any clients until the next day. I breathed a sigh of relief. I wasn't up to seeing any clients. I knew I'd still be distracted with April's murder, except now it was all about saving Joey from Estelle.

I heard a knock on my door and wondered who it could be. As I looked through the peephole Jesse had insisted I get, I saw my contractor, Abe Larson. He was probably around fifty years old, had a full head of sandy blonde hair, was medium height, maybe six inches taller than me, and even though he wasn't that handsome, when his smile lit up his face he became very attractive. His standard uniform was typical of contractors who got their hands dirty on site, which made his physique even more attractive, being able to see his bulging biceps come out of his t-shirts.

I opened the door to my office and realized that I had actually forgotten he had been at my main house, that's how distracted April's murder made me.

"Hi, Abe, come on in. What's happening? Where are we?"

"You haven't even been in the place, have you?" He accused.

I had the decency to look embarrassed as I shook my head no.

"MJ, the house looks fantastic. All we need to do is get the paint colors you want and we'll be finished, with just a few minor issues. Can you walk through with me today? Now would be preferred."

I inhaled a deep breath and told him to just give me a few minutes and I'd be right out.

After he left, I sat in my therapy chair and started doing my breathing just like I was taught until the internal shaking subsided. I'd been in the house hundreds of times as they were rebuilding, so I didn't know why I was so shaken up about it now that it was almost finished.

April's murder definitely had triggered my PTSD response and I needed to hang on to something that made me believe I was in control. This is what I learned from my trauma therapist. Find a focal point, one that I had some control over.

The first thing that came to mind was focusing on Jesse, but that was a red herring because I had absolutely no control over him and what he did or didn't do. But thinking about him made me feel safe. He was the kind of person who would jump in and protect me and anyone else who needed protecting without worry to self. That's why he was a cop.

So instead of following my trauma therapist's advice, I thought about Jesse, and calmed myself down immediately. To hell with trying to deny my feelings for him.

Abe met me at the back door of the house, clipboard in hand. I marveled at how much had been done since the last time I had walked through. It all looked so new. It seemed to sparkle; since it was all so white from the sheet rock.

The room where the fire had started and where I had almost lost my life was the back room, the one that had the sliding glass and screen doors. Instead of a therapy room, they had turned it into a back porch that I would be able to close off to the cooler weather in the winter and to have it totally open in the summer.

I loved it and it had absolutely nothing about it that reminded me of what the room was before. I had told the architect to make it into something interesting that was open to the elements, and was not really a room, but an open air porch. I didn't want the space to remind me of what happened in that room. It was also the room that had been earmarked for the baby's room, which we never had.

We continued to walk through the little house and I was delighted at how open it was. Every room had either an opening to the outside, or a skylight that let the light in. I'm prone to depression during the winter months and need the sun to counter it. This was all perfect. The architect had done a splendid job and Abe had tweaked a few things for me that made it an absolute dream.

When we were through, I threw my arms around him and told him I was delighted and wanted him and his wife over for dinner when it was finally completed.

He seemed a little embarrassed by my display of affection, but gladly accepted it and went on to ask what I wanted to do about the landscaping.

I honestly hadn't even thought about it. I was going into debt with just the rebuild. I didn't think I could actually do anything about the landscape for several years and told him that.

He didn't press me and told me to give him a call when I was ready to go deeper into debt and he'd give me his opinion on whom I should hire. He then went on to tell me a few things I could do in order to make the yard look at least presentable, which I appreciated. I thanked him for the information.

The last thing we had to do was to pick the color of the paints for each room. I was not that good at decorating, so I deferred to him. If my memory served me, I thought he had picked the colors for Franny's place in Santa Monica and it was lovely. I just didn't have the bandwidth to figure out colors with everything going on with Aunt Carrie and Joey.

After he left, I pulled out an old lawn chair from the back and put it in the open air porch and just sat there looking out at my backyard. The only living thing out there was the little lemon tree I had planted after my husband, Gideon, had died. I hadn't given it much attention lately, but it seemed to be thriving. It had some lemons on it and I hadn't even noticed.

As I sat and fantasized about how I could furnish my open air porch, the scenes of the night Mike Rimichi almost strangled me to death came back. Visions of my client crashing through the glass windows came and then me picking up the crowbar and swinging at Mike's head seemed to repeat over and over.

I forced my eyes open and instead of the place being on fire, I saw the open space and felt the warmth of the day soak into my body. I could hear the nearby workers shouting to each other and I stood up, telling myself it was only a dream. But I wondered if I would ever be able to live comfortably in the main house again. I knew that April's murder had reopened all the terror of that night when I killed Mike Rimichi.

Chapter 26

Sunday had arrived and as I got ready to go to April's memorial, I dressed carefully, knowing Jesse was going to be there. The healthy part of me knew I was playing with fire, but the yearning and needy part seemed to be taking over more and more.

It was starting again, all the obsessing and yearning and wanting from him. I knew, because Big Al told me, that getting involved with him could trigger me into drinking again.

I told myself that I wasn't getting involved with him. That he was just someone I knew who had an inside with the investigation of April's murder and he could be helpful to Aunt Carrie.

Who was I kidding? I would have taken any opportunity to see him, to be in the same room as him. I knew it was threatening my sobriety, but I didn't care. I mean, April was murdered, what could be worse than that? Why was I worried about slipping and having a drink?

Big Al would say that kind of thinking is stinkin' thinkin', and I was sick of those phrases. But I was still going to meetings and I hadn't had a drink yet. So maybe it's not as bad as he thinks.

I told Big Al about April's memorial, but he declined, saying that he didn't know her and felt like it was more of a private memorial for those closest to her.

I understood. He was right. I just wanted him there to keep me on the straight and narrow. Aunt Carrie had ordered chardonnay for people to drink. I liked chardonnay and was worried that I may have a glass or two.

I wore a simple dark cotton dress with black open-toed sandals. I pulled my curly dark hair away from my face with hair combs and applied my make-up with care.

I arrived early in order to help Aunt Carrie set up chairs. It was going to be out on the patio and because of the hot weather we were having, she had scheduled it for later afternoon around 4 pm. But it was still going to be hot and the sun was still quite high at that hour.

The caterers had already arrived and had tables with white tablecloths and extra umbrellas to keep the sun off of the guests. I hadn't needed to be there to help set up chairs because the caterers had already done that.

The patio looked pretty with all of Aunt Carrie's colorful summer flowers in bloom in the garden and surrounding the patio. It couldn't have been more beautiful. And so much better than a stodgy, dark and gloomy funeral home.

Little Joey was running around helping the caterers and since most of them were college age, they were pleasant with her and let her help in little ways. She had used her artistic skills to do some drawings for her mother's memorial and they were plastered wherever there was an open space to scotch tape them.

I took my iPhone out of my purse and started taking snapshots. I wanted Joey to have beautiful memories of this affair. It looked like there was a party about to happen.

Guests started to arrive a little before four and I helped meet and greet them, showing them where the drinks and food were, and asking them how they knew April.

Most of them were either neighbors or from her school. A few were parents of some of the students that she taught. They seemed the most distraught and I wondered what they had told their children about why April was no longer at school. I didn't even know what the teachers were telling the students.

After everyone had gotten some food and something to drink, they started forming little groups and were talking in low tones. I noticed that the caterers were making their way around the guests, filling their wine glasses and offering plates of little snacks. If I didn't know this was a memorial, I would have thought it was a garden party, except most people wore dark or black clothing.

There was one large photo of April next to the food table. I had no idea when Aunt Carrie had done that. I wondered when she had had the time to do all of this. But, I knew it was good for her. She wanted to do the best for her child. It would be the last time she did anything for April.

Finally, Aunt Carrie clapped her hands and invited everyone to sit down. The chairs had been arranged in a circle so everyone could see each other. She stood up in front of everyone and thanked them all for coming.

She then asked if people wanted to share their memories or any stories they had about April. By this time it was close to 5 pm and the heat of the sun was starting to lessen a bit. The shade of the trees helped people from having to shade their eyes and I saw Joey standing close behind her grandmother.

One by one, the guests shared. It was poignant and people laughed and cried.

Finally, little Joey stood up and walked into the middle of the circle and said in a loud and clear voice. "It's my turn to talk about my mommy."

There was total stillness and no one said a word. All eyes were on this little girl who had just lost her mother by a brutal murderer.

She twirled around making her party dress swirl around her little legs and then she started singing a song in Spanish, clapping her hands, and moving in cute little dance steps. As she continued, we all got in the mood and started clapping to the rhythm of her song.

When she was done, she stopped and pronounced, "This was for my mommy. She taught me this song and I made up the dance. I love you Mommy."

She didn't cry, but the rest of us were weeping into our tissues that the caterers had cleverly thought to bring and had passed around.

It seemed like Joey's sharing would end the memorial, because who could really say anything that would sound like anything at all once Joey had completed her song and dance?

Everyone sat in total silent, no one daring to be the first one to move or speak. Then, as if out of a Grimes fairy tale, the light seemed to dim, a whirl of wind spun some dried up flowers, and two figures entered the garden, casting a dark energy to the whole proceedings.

It was Estelle and Benjamin.

Chapter 27

They weren't alone. There was a middle-aged man who came up right behind them. He was dressed in a very expensive looking suit. Since I could never afford expensive labels, I had no idea what they were, but his fitted him to perfection and I could see an expensive looking watch on his left wrist and I knew immediately he was their lawyer.

I didn't need to be psychic to know that they weren't there to share memories about April, and I knew something bad was about to happen. They were here for Joey. I got up quickly and took Joey by the hand, and so I wouldn't scare her, I ushered her into the house. I wondered why Jesse hadn't arrived. He would know what to do in this situation. He was law enforcement. He wouldn't allow them to take her. He couldn't.

I grabbed my phone and texted him, asking where he was and if he was coming or not.

He immediately texted back that he was on his way and had gotten delayed but would be there shortly.

I sat with Joey in the kitchen, surrounded by the caterers. I had no idea what was happening outside on the patio, and I didn't really want to know.

But just then, the lawyer came inside and went straight to Joey. "Come with me, Joey," he ordered.

"You aren't taking her anywhere." I tried to act like I knew what I was doing, but it was a bluff. In my mind I was praying for Jesse to hurry.

Aunt Carrie came in holding a piece of paper and held it out to me and said, "They've managed to do it, MJ. This paper says they have the legal right to be Joey's guardian. I need to call my lawyer."

What happened next was like something out of a terrible movie. Estelle came in and went directly to Joey, plucked her out of her chair and started carrying her out the back door.

Joey kicked and screamed but was no match for Estelle. I saw Franny outside walking toward the frightened child. Seeing her shook me out of my shocked stupor and I raced out the door toward Joey and Estelle.

Benjamin did nothing to help Estelle, but he didn't do anything to help little Joey either. Where the hell was Jesse? Someone needed to put a stop to this madness. They couldn't just come and kidnap her in front of all these witnesses. Legal paper be damned.

Franny and I got to Joey at the same time and as we both reached out our arms to grab her, total chaos erupted. The entire pack of people at the memorable started surrounding Estelle and Joey, with Fanny and I pulling at Joey to get Estelle to release her.

I could see people taking out their cellphones to film the scene and there was shouting coming from the entire garden. Everyone was telling Estelle to leave Joey alone.

It was like a nightmare. I started to feel crushed by the bodies pushing up against me. I tried to tell them to back up, that they were doing more harm than good, but it had gone too far. All the anger and grief about the murder of April was erupting from people who were normally quite civilized.

Suddenly it all stopped when I heard a loud, shrill whistle. Everyone froze and Estelle let go of Joey as Franny and I held her close.

Jesse had finally arrived. He saw the chaos, but didn't understand what was happening.

"I want everyone to stand down, NOW!" He bellowed.

I felt more than saw the crowd move back away from us.

"What the hell is going on?"

I saw him search me out and then stared at me with a question. By this point, I was sitting on the ground holding Joey on my lap trying to calm her down. Aunt Carrie ran up to us and tried to sit down too, but it was too difficult for her with her added weight and I saw Franny bring a chair for her. Joey went into her lap and snuggled into her bosom and cried loudly between hiccups, telling us all that she wanted to stay with her nana.

Estelle spoke first. "We have every legal right to take this child into our possession. You are all interfering with that right. Now, everyone back away and let us do what we came to do."

Just the way Estelle was going about taking Joey without preparing her, and even worse, taking her at her mother's memorial, proved that she was one of the worst people to be raising Joey. Where was Marilyn Parks, the social worker? Where was Child Protective Service? How could this have happened?

What little I knew about the family court system was that they put the child first. Aunt Carrie's lawyer also stated that's the way it worked. What the hell went wrong here? Were the Sparks that influential? Did they have that much power in the legal system? It didn't seem possible. But here they were with a legal document saying they were the legal guardians.

"Jesse, you have to do something. They're here to take Joey. They have some kind of legal document saying they're her legal guardians. Do something."

I could hear my voice getting more and more shrill. I could tell I was about to lose it.

Jesse came over and held out his hand for the document, which Aunt Carrie relinquished.

After reading it, he looked up helplessly and said, "It looks like they are the legal guardians. There isn't anything I can do at this moment, but Carrie, you better call your lawyer. He'll know what to do."

He then turned to Estelle and without rancor said, "You ought to be ashamed of yourself, coming to a memorial service with a paper that you knew would upset everyone, especially that little girl. I pray that you lose custody, but also your rights to even see her. Now, give her real grandma some time with her to console her and prepare her to go with you. You and your lawyer need to wait out in the car. We'll let you know when Joey is ready to go."

Estelle, without her funeral hat, looked more and more like Cruella de Vil. I hadn't noticed before, but she had a white streak going down the left side of her head; the rest of her hair was black, turning to gray.

I disliked her for what she was attempting to do, but without her austere black clothing and veil, her slimness looked more unhealthy than that of someone who was watching their weight. This along with her pale and drawn face, I considered that she might actually be sick, or even dying. She did not look healthy at all.

We all watched in silence as she considered what Jesse had asked her to do. She finally turned and snapped her fingers for Benjamin and the lawyer to follow her out.

There was a collective breath of relief and we all started talking at once. I turned to Aunt Carrie and told her that she needed to call her lawyer first. He needed to stop this before Estelle got hold of Joey.

Joey was still nestled in her nana's lap. I asked Aunt Carrie where her phone was so I could bring it to her, but Franny stepped in and stated that she'd call him and try to get him here ASAP, before Estelle lost her patience and demanded Joey.

I could see Estelle calling more cops, or demanding that Jesse make us give Joey to her. I knew policemen have no other option than to enforce legal documents when it came to child custody and I knew it would kill Jesse to enforce this one.

The memorial crowd was hovering around and asking what they could do. I went and got a piece of paper and pen and asked them all to please write their name and number down in case we needed them as witnesses. I then thanked them all for coming and making the memorial into a beautiful event until Estelle showed up. I acknowledged all of their support and reminded all of us, including myself, that it had been a wonderful memorial service and what happened at the end could not take that away.

After everyone supplied their name and numbers, one by one they filtered out of the patio. I looked at my phone to see how much time had passed and asked Franny if the lawyer was able to come.

He told her that he wasn't able to come right away, but to scan and send him the legal document, and he'd see what he could do.

Once he got the copy of the document, the bad news came. He told Franny we'd have to relinquish Joey for now, but that he was on it.

"NO WAY!" I shouted when I heard the news, "There is no way Joey's leaving us."

"MJ, please," Aunt Carrie pleaded, "don't make it worse than it already is. We need to prepare Joey to be taken by them. Please, tone it down and let's help her cope."

I was embarrassed by my inability to contain myself. Of course, Joey came first. I needed to stay calm for her, and for Aunt Carrie. My love for Joey and Aunt Carrie made it very personal and I could feel myself slipping into a very bad place. I looked over at the leftover wine and knew I needed to get myself back under control.

I knew what I had to do. I called Big Al.

Chapter 28

After he congratulated me for not drinking the wine, he helped me calm down and look at the situation rationally. It made sense to prepare Joey for the inevitable. We all needed to be strong and calm for the little girl, as she prepared to leave all she knew to go be with strangers.

When I was calm, he asked me what, as a psychologist, I thought would be the best course of action to take with a little four-year-old.

I took a breath and detached myself from the personal emotions I was feeling and told Big Al that I thought if we phrased it in a way that would seem like an adventure to Joey, that could work, since she was such an adventurous child. She was very social and didn't seem shy around strangers. We needed to somehow hide our feelings toward Estelle and Benjamin and tell Joey that they loved her and wanted to get to know her too, since they were her other grandparents.

So that is what we did. Joey perked up and she and Aunt Carrie went into her room to pack some of her clothes and toys. She came out carrying her cock-eyed Lucy Bear, grinning.

"MJ, I'm taking Lucy with me because she wants an adventure too. Can we get ice cream?"

"I don't know, Sweetie, we'll ask your grandparents if they could stop and get you an ice cream cone, okay?"

I then knelt down and drew her close to me and gave her a big hug as I whispered into her ear, "If you get scared, stay close to Grandpa. He's a nice man and you can trust him."

I didn't know if this was true, but I got a feeling that he was mortified at what they had come to do on the day of April's memorial. He had looked stricken with shame. Maybe he'd be able to stand up for Joey, or at least be someone Joey could go to for comfort. Lord knew she'd need it.

It was Jesse, I think, who went to bring Estelle and Benjamin back in. Since he was the most neutral of all of us, he suggested to them that they might entice Joey with the promise of an ice cream cone.

Estelle made an ugly face, but then gave a fake smile and said to Joey, "Of course, Joey, we can get you an ice cream, isn't that right, Benji?"

After all the bravado in preparing Joey, when it came to actually taking Estelle's hand when they left, she hesitated and looked back for support, then ran back and hugged her nana, who couldn't help but hug her tightly for a long time, tears in her eyes.

We all managed a smile as Joey left with the Sparks. I swear I'll never forget the look on her face as she looked back at all of us as Estelle led her away.

After they were gone, we all started talking at once. Everyone had a different opinion on what our next step should be. But we were all in agreement that the number one priority was to get Joey back as soon as possible.

Franny finally had the most logical answer when she said, "Let's let Peter study the document first to see if there is any loophole in it. He's a really good lawyer. If he can't figure something out, then there won't be any legal way of getting her back."

"What are you saying, Franny?"

"Carrie, what I'm saying is that if we can't figure out a way of getting Joey back that's legal, then we're going to have to figure out some other way."

"Like what?" I asked.

"I don't know. We'll have to put our imaginations together and find another way."

Jesse stood at this and said, "If you guys are talking about something illegal, I'm going to have to leave. I can't be a part of this."

The rest of us looked at each other, knowing full well we were all thinking we'd do whatever it took.

"Oh, no, Jesse," I heard Franny lie, "we wouldn't think of anything illegal, but just in case one of us says something that could be interpreted as illegal, maybe you should go."

"I'll see you to the door," I said.

There was complete silence as I walked Jesse out the door.

When we were alone, he turned to me and said, "Promise me you won't do anything rash, MJ. I know how attached you all are to that kid, but trust me, it's not worth it."

"Oh, yeah, that's right, you were being investigated by your own department for breaking some rules before you got shot. That's why you came to me in the first place for therapy. How did all that pan out?"

We had never addressed that after he recovered from the three shots he took when he got in the crosshairs of Detective Slatter, aka Mike Rimichi, the kingpin for the illegal sales of steroids and other narcotics.

He leaned in toward me, a grim look on his face and said, "I'm not kidding, MJ. I won't be able to protect you. I was lucky and got away with it, but you're an open book and not a very good liar. Keep your nose clean, or at the very least make very sure you don't get caught. And have that lawyer guy, Peter, on speed dial."

He turned and walked away. I was a little confused. Was he warning me that if we did something illegal, he would know and he'd book us himself? Or was he giving me his blessing to do whatever I need to do, but don't get caught.

When I went back inside, the consensus was to wait for Peter and I had to agree. It was getting late and the caterers had already cleaned up and were gone, so there was nothing more to do.

Aunt Carrie suggested that Franny and I go home and try to get a good night's sleep, although we knew that was going to be impossible.

"I don't want to leave you, Aunt Carrie. Don't you think I should stay here with you tonight?"

"No, MJ, you go on home. I'm going to need you in the next week or so and I want you to take care of yourself now."

She used her hands to make a shooing motion, so Franny and I left together.

"Want to go get a dri. . . .coffee or something?"

"Yeah, I'd love to go get a drink with you, Franny. But I'm not going to. I need my wits about me if we're going to try and figure all of this out, and besides I'm coming up on four months of sobriety. I'm kind of looking forward to getting another chip.

She laughed and asked if I'd like some company for a while. I told her that I was okay, that I'd call her tomorrow and then I thanked her for being so helpful. It felt like old times again. When the chips were down, Franny did come through. It's just that when there weren't any chips, she was kind of self-centered.

Chapter 29

Alone in my flat, I looked around and saw that there was still Joey paraphernalia lying around and it made me sad. I straightened up and put her things in a small brown bag and hid it on the top shelf in my tiny kitchenette. I couldn't stand to see it. I had wanted to go into my denial mode, which was getting harder and harder to do since I had quit drinking.

It was only 9 p.m., so I took my iPad and opened it to find something to watch to take my mind off what had just happened. Nothing looked good, so I turned it off and sat worrying about Joey. I wondered how she was. Did they get her ice cream or was Estelle just being a manipulative psychopath, promising her things, but then not doing it?

I realized that I was being unfair to Estelle. I didn't really know her. She just seemed so entitled and smug, which, I have to admit, intimidated me. I grew up poor and people with money always seemed elusive to me. Maybe I needed to get to know her to see what kind of a person she really was. She was so skinny. So again, I wondered if maybe she was dying of cancer or some other terrible disease.

My mind started analyzing what I knew about April's murder. It's something I do all the time with my clients. I'd take what they told me and then analyze what didn't make sense and try to come up with various scenarios that did make sense based on what they told me.

Big Al's voice kept creeping in as I took one of my legal pads and started writing down what I knew. He'd tell me that it wasn't my job to figure out who killed April. I should let the police do their job. He would tell me that I can't fix everything, or make it right for everyone.

I ignored his voice as much as I could and started writing, first what I knew as facts:

-April was strangled with some kind of a belt.

-It happened late at night or early morning.

-She was found in her backyard leaning against her locked door, so she had locked the door behind her, but the fact that she had openly stepped outside indicated that she knew the person but didn't trust them.

-There was no evidence left behind, which I assumed to mean, no DNA or clothing, or anything else that could either be from Alex, or a stranger.

-Alex was missing. He vanished without a trace.

-His parents had Joey and they had gone to great lengths to get her.

-April was well liked and had no enemies besides Alex.

I then wrote down what I did not know:

-I did not know where Alex was.

-I did not know why his parents were so intent on getting Joey after ignoring her from birth.

-I did not know how Estelle's lawyer was able to get legal guardianship of Joey.

- I did not know who killed April. If Alex didn't do it, I did not know who else would have had a motive to kill her.

When I wrote the last item, I knew where it was I needed to start. The only lead I had was from Aunt Carrie when she talked about April befriending her teenage neighbor. Even though the police had ruled him out as a suspect, my instinct told me that he might know something. Kids and teens often knew things about the adults around them that the adults were sure they were hiding.

He hadn't been at the memorial service and I didn't know if his parents had been there or not. I hadn't been paying attention to that particular piece of information. However, we had asked all the people at the memorial to give us their name and number, so I was sure I would be able to find out the number of that kid through the contacts we got.

I looked at my phone. It was nearing midnight, so I had to wait until morning to go over to Aunt Carrie's house and get the numbers.

I yawned and started to feel the fatigue caused by such an emotional day. Knowing what my next step was, relaxed me and I was able to fall asleep quickly, my mind at rest for a change. I didn't even give Jesse a moment's thought, and I was able to stop my worry over Joey. I knew in my heart that we'd find April's killer and somehow the lawyer Aunt Carrie hired would find a way to get Joey back where she belonged.

At least that's what I told myself.

Chapter 30

I actually woke up before the sun streamed into my windows, but I could tell that the heat of the day was already beginning. We had been in a really long heat wave and I was tired of it. I like the warm, but not the hot.

I made my coffee a double and let it cool while I took my shower and dressed in my uniform of the day, a tank top and shorts.

At 6 a.m., I figured Aunt Carrie would be awake, so I hustled over to her place and walked into the kitchen where I found her sitting at the table drinking a cup of coffee.

When she looked up at me, she gave a half-hearted smile. She had bags under her eyes and I knew she most likely hadn't slept much. I knew she'd be worried about Joey and was still grieving about April. I'm not sure which would be worse.

I shook my head no when she indicated for me to get a cup of coffee. I had already had my double for the morning and her coffee was too bitter. I had gotten used to it when I had lived with her after my house burned down, but was making my own now and didn't think I could handle another cup.

"Aunt Carrie, I need the sheet of paper where people put their name and numbers from the memorial yesterday. Where did you put it?"

She sat there with a look of confusion on her face.

"Remember, we asked everyone to write their name and number in case we needed them as witnesses against the Sparks?"

"Oh, yes, I vaguely remember something like that happening."

"Do you know where it is?" I started looking around the kitchen, opening drawers and lifting up dishes on the table to see if it got caught beneath anything.

"Aunt Carrie, focus, please. I need to get the number of that kid April befriended."

"Why would you need his number?"

"Call it a hunch. I thought of it last night when I was making lists of things we knew and didn't know about April's murder. I think that kid might know something. I have a feeling the police didn't really interrogate him. They probably got his alibi and left it at that. He's just a teenager. I don't think he was ever a serious suspect, but adults don't take kids and teens seriously. I'm guessing he may know something that may be important but wasn't asked by the authorities."

I watched her sit and drink her coffee, a puzzled look on her face. She was starting to annoy me; I needed those numbers and she was acting like she was sleepwalking, or sleep sitting.

If I had the ability to snap my fingers, I would have snapped them in front of her face. I grabbed her arm and looked into her eyes and said, "Aunt Carrie, focus."

She got up and slowly started to help me search for the missing sheet of paper with the names and numbers. As we looked around the kitchen, it was apparent it wasn't there, so we started looking in the rest of the house. We became more and more frantic as we searched and could not find it.

"Damn it." I finally admitted it wasn't in the house. Then, I wondered if someone had taken it. Could one of the Sparks or their lawyer have gotten hold of it? Or Franny, maybe? I remembered seeing it on one of the tables from the caterers and realized that they probably threw it away as trash when they were putting their gear away and moving it out to their van.

I went to the kitchen garbage and rummaged through it, but didn't find anything, so I forced myself to take a look in the outside garbage bin.

Nothing.

Okay, I had to think. I didn't really need that sheet of paper. It would have made life easier if I had it, but I decided that I'd just go over to April's house and start knocking on doors to see if someone knew where the teen lived.

I told Aunt Carrie what I was going to do and she asked if I'd like her to come with me. She looked so sad and out of it that I told her that I didn't need her with me, that it was probably a wild goose chase anyway. I told her that she looked tired and thought it might be a good idea if she stayed and tried to get some rest.

When I got to April's neighborhood, I parked my car in front of her house. I saw that they had finally taken the yellow tape down and it looked normal again. I looked up and down the street and decided that I'd start with the two houses next to hers. It was early on Monday morning and I hoped that people were still home and hadn't gone into work yet. Otherwise, it would be difficult for me to find that young man.

There was no answer from the two houses right next door, but I hit the jackpot on the third try, a couple of houses down from April's.

A middle-aged woman, still dressed in a bathrobe, answered the door. She still had sleep in her eyes and looked out at me in recognition.

"Oh, hey, you were at April's memorial yesterday. What a day, right?" Then she looked confused and asked why I was there.

I introduced myself and then told her that we had lost the sheet of paper where people had written their names and numbers. I apologized for waking her and then explained that I was looking for a young man or a teenager that April had befriended.

"You came to the right place, MJ," then called out loud, "Jimmy, someone is here to see you."

She turned back to me and told me how the police had come to ask about Jimmy. She told me that Jimmy had been at home that entire night, then went on to explain that he was on the spectrum, so even though he was already seventeen years old, he acted a lot younger and still needed parental supervision. She said he was getting some help through social services, but had been integrated into regular school.

She leaned toward me and spoke in almost a whisper which was difficult for me to hear. She said something to the effect that he wasn't normal like the other kids and he often got bullied. April had tried to help him deal with it and looked out for him at school, especially during lunchtime. "I don't know how he's going to get by next year without her. He'll be a senior. He's smart in a lot of ways, you know? He just has a hard time socializing. Breaks my heart to see it, but I love him. What do you need to talk to him about, if I may ask?"

Jimmy's mother was talkative and I began to think that she also might have some extra knowledge about April and who April may or may not have been seeing. It looked like she was a stay-at-home mom, most likely stayed at home with her special needs son, was very friendly and I assumed liked to gossip and may know a lot of things in the neighborhood.

"As you know," I began.

"Where are my manners? Come on inside. I haven't even had my coffee yet. Excuse the robe. I sleep in during the summer months because Jimmy doesn't have school. He likes to sleep in later than usual too, so we indulge ourselves. Come on in."

I stepped inside to a house that felt cozy and warm. She led me to the kitchen and had me sit on a bar stool that was one of four around the kitchen island.

As she hustled about, she reminded me of Aunt Carrie: a bit overweight, jolly and happy, down to earth, and one might say 'salt of the earth.'

"Is Jimmy still sleeping?"

"Probably. It takes an act of god to wake him if he's stayed up late working on one of his projects. Once he gets interested in something, he can't let it go. Are you familiar with autism, MJ?"

"A little bit. I'm a psychologist and have some knowledge of it, but it's not my expertise."

After she made sure the coffee was dripping through the filter, she excused herself and told me she was going to go wake the boy up, that it was time he was up anyway.

I looked around at the cozy kitchen and felt comforted. I wondered if there was a father around, or other siblings. As I sat on the barstool, I suddenly felt like I was being watched and turned to see a young boy standing at the doorway looking intently at me.

"You startled me," I said.

He was a bit taller than me, but still seemed short as if he hadn't hit his growth spurt yet. His hair was combed and it looked like he had slicked it down with some kind of gel. His clothes were casual and worn, blue jeans and a t-shirt that had a picture of a cartoon dog on it.

I smiled and held out my hand and said, "Hi, I'm MJ. You must be Jimmy. It's nice to meet you."

He came fully into the kitchen without acknowledging me and went to the cupboard, found a box of cheerios and poured them into a large bowl. At the refrigerator, he poured a generous amount of milk into the bowl. Much more milk than was needed for the amount of cereal. He came and sat next to me as he ate, crunching the toasted cheerios that hadn't yet gone soggy from the milk.

Hmmm, I thought to myself, this was going to be harder than I thought. I wished his mother would come back to help me talk to him. I didn't know how severe his autism was, but if he had been integrated into a regular school, it couldn't be that severe.

The coffee kept dripping into the pot until the pot was full. Jimmy kept crunching his cereal, and I just sat there waiting.

I wanted to start asking him a bunch of questions, but somehow it felt wrong to do that with this kid. He looked smaller than his years, more like a twelve-year-old than a seventeen-year-old. It was hard to believe he would be a senior next school year.

His mother finally came back. She had changed into a loose fitting housedress, combed her hair and I could see she had applied some ultra red lipstick. It made her look rather comical, but I didn't laugh. She seemed like a real character.

I started to say her name and then realized I didn't know it, so instead I asked her, "I'm sorry, I don't even know your name."

"Oh my, I'm always doing that. I just start in talking. I've been told that I'm too casual and it will get me into trouble someday, but so far it hasn't."

"So you are?"

"Oh, yes, my name is Nancy, Nancy Friday. And you know my son Jimmy Friday."

"Would it be okay if I asked you both some questions?"

"That's why you're here, isn't it?"

"Well, yes, but I want to make sure you are both okay with it."

She went over to her coffee pot and poured herself a generous cup of coffee. I had never seen such a large coffee cup. She added several spoons of sugar, reached into the refrigerator, took the milk Jimmy had just used, poured it in her coffee, and stirred.

After taking a large noisy sip of her coffee, she poured me a cup and asked if I wanted milk or sugar.

I took the cup and told her that black was fine, then asked them both what the police had asked them.

Nancy didn't seem concerned at all about why the police had come to her house asking about her son Jimmy. Watching them both, I realized that there was no way this skinny little special-needs kid had murdered April. Whoever murdered April was a lot stronger than he was and most likely taller too. Jimmy couldn't have been any taller than five feet, four or five inches.

Basically, they had just asked where Jimmy was that night. His mother was pretty clear he was in bed early that night and had woken her up around 5:30 a.m., asking her where she had put his project he had been working on. It had annoyed her because she was still tired, but she had gotten up and found the thing, deciding not to go back to bed.

Since they lived a couple of houses down from April, I asked them both if they had noticed anything unusual at her house, seen any strangers, or anything out of the ordinary.

Nancy hadn't noticed, but then told me that Jimmy wouldn't answer questions from me if I talked to him like I was.

I asked for her help in questioning him and she took over. It was fascinating to watch her interact with her son. She asked him who else came to April's house.

"Joey lives there with April."

"Yes, Joey does live there with April, Jimmy. Did another person come to visit April when you were there?"

"I didn't hurt April."

"I know, Jimmy, of course you didn't. You liked Ms. April."

"April's dead."

"Yes, Jimmy, April's dead."

I had a strange impression that Jimmy may have seen April dead, so I interjected, "Jimmy, I know April was nice to you. How did you know April got hurt?"

"I saw her eyes."

"What about her eyes?"

"They didn't blink. We have to blink our eyes. It keeps them moist. If we don't blink, we could lose our eyesight. She didn't blink her eyes, so I knew she couldn't see."

"You saw her lying in her backyard?"

He looked at his mother, who told him that he could answer the question. She told him he wasn't in trouble and he could tell what he saw.

"I saw her with her eyes open, not blinking. I got scared, so I ran home."

"Did you see another person around?"

"There were a bunch of people with her, but Joey wasn't there."

I turned to Nancy and asked her if she knew any of this to which she replied it was all new to her.

It seemed that Jimmy had gone over to April's early in the morning to find some watercolors he had left in her backyard and saw April with her eyes open. The police were there already and he had gotten scared and had run back home.

I wasn't sure if Jimmy knew anything more, but clearly seeing April dead with her eyes open had spooked him. I wondered if we had gotten all he knew about April and her life, or any visitors she may have had.

I tried again, "Jimmy, besides all the policemen who were there when April's eyes were open, were there any other strangers you might have seen at her house before April died? Like any time before? Was April scared or upset at any time that you can remember?"

"April cried. She understood that I was sad when the other kids bullied me. She told me that Alex bullied her and it made her sad."

"Okay, did you ever see Alex? Do you know what he looks like?"

"No, Alex is not allowed to come see April anymore. He was bad and he can't see her."

"That's right, Jimmy. Were there any other strangers that came to see April that you can remember?"

"There weren't any strangers."

I was disappointed. Talking to Jimmy seemed like a dead-end to me. I asked Nancy if she saw any strangers at April's house and she also told me that she hadn't seen anyone there other than Joey and Carrie Pedersen.

I gave Nancy my card and asked her to call me if she heard anything from any of the neighbors. I was pretty sure she'd probably gossip with them about me coming over and would quiz them. Being a gossip, she'd probably get more out of her neighbors than I would.

I had been so sure my intuition was correct about Jimmy. I guess I was wrong. I don't see how he could have done it. He was so small and likable. But I did think that he might have more information than he was giving us, but probably didn't even know he had it. I decided that I may have to circle around again to see if there was more information to get from him.

Chapter 31

As I left April's neighborhood, the day grew more and more hot and even my car A/C seemed not to be able to keep the heat out. If I hadn't been so coffee'd up, I would have stopped at a Starbucks and gotten a Frappuccino. This would have been the perfect day to take Joey for an ice cream cone. I would have enjoyed one with her. Just the thought of her with Estelle made me furious.

I had been so sure Jimmy was going to reveal something important that I didn't have another plan. So it was back to the drawing board.

The heat was making me tired and grouchy, so I decided to head back to my place and try and get some work done. I couldn't put my life on hold, because I still needed to make a living.

But first I decided to call Franny to see if Peter had made any progress on fighting Estelle's legal custody documents.

She answered on the first ring, but no, there wasn't anything definitive about how to combat Estelle's manipulation. Franny told me that Peter couldn't understand how the Sparks could have gotten custody. It went against everything he knew and understood about the family courts. He thought that they must have had some kind of pull that he couldn't see.

This proved to only make me more furious. I was beside myself with fury with no place to go with it.

The day didn't get any better when I stopped in to check with Aunt Carrie. She told me that Detective Myer called and told her that they still couldn't find any trace of Alex, nor did they have any other leads on who could have murdered her daughter.

How could someone get murdered and there be absolutely no evidence and no leads? Actually, Alex was a suspect, but he had completely vanished.

We were all missing something. But what?

The police apparently had looked into Alex getting fake identification. They had checked out all known forgers of fake ID's and nothing came up. What that said to me was that someone must have set him up for the murder, then got rid of him. Or, he had a partner who would benefit by April's death.

"Aunt Carrie, do you know if Alex was seeing anyone?"

"You mean, like another woman?"

"Exactly, did he have a girlfriend that you know of?"

"I don't think so. April never said anything about another woman. I guess he could have gotten one after they split up, but he was pretty fixated on April, so I doubt it."

"Do you know of anyone who would know for sure? Like a buddy of his?"

"What are you trying to say, MJ?"

"What if he had a partner in crime? Let's say he murdered April, and had a girlfriend who helped him by picking him up in her car and taking him someplace where he wouldn't be caught. Maybe they planned the whole thing and either he had saved up a bunch of cash or maybe his girlfriend was wealthy."

Aunt Carrie gave out a short burst of what sounded kind of like a laugh, but was more of a snort. "I know you're trying to help, MJ, but what could possibly be a motive for a girlfriend?"

I had to think about it for a while, and truthfully, I really couldn't come up with anything. It wasn't to get Joey because Alex already had 50% custody which meant he didn't have to pay any child support, and they hadn't been married, so there wasn't any alimony to pay out.

"You're right, Aunt Carrie, I can't think of any motive, but still, I'd like to check it out. Do you know of any of his buddies? Or, where he worked?"

She knew she couldn't stop me from going down that rabbit hole, so she went and got her address book. She used a paper address book since she didn't use her smartphone very much. It was just easier for her to keep everyone she knew in her address book. She had told me it would take too long to transfer everyone into her phone.

After looking through the book, she finally found what she was looking for. It was a mutual friend of Alex and April. Her name was Amy Williams. Aunt Carrie told me that she was the only friend of April's that Alex allowed her to see, mainly because he liked her too.

I wondered if Amy might be his new girlfriend. Maybe she couldn't have kids and was in love with Joey and wanted them to be a family. I've heard worse stories. Being a psychologist, sometimes I think I've heard it all, and then someone comes in and surprises me with something even more unbelievable.

I took Amy's number and gave her a call. She did not answer, so I left a voice message asking her to please call me and that it was urgent.

Aunt Carrie looked at me with mournful eyes and shook her head, "MJ, you can't fix this. I'm not sure anyone can."

That's what everyone was telling me. That I couldn't 'fix it.' But I couldn't give up either. I didn't think I could live next door to Aunt Carrie, seeing her almost every day, hurting like she was, living without Joey. I didn't think I would be able to bear it. Plus, I thought that if she didn't get Joey back and she couldn't get grandparent rights, she might move back to the Midwest. I wasn't sure which would be harder for me.

Was I being selfish? Maybe, but Aunt Carrie was my family, and April and Joey had become my family, too. I had fallen in love with that little girl and I had to get her away from Estelle. It wouldn't be healthy for her to live with that psychopath.

I had to find a way to get Joey back. In my mind, I felt that there was a connection somehow between finding April's murder and getting Joey back. Maybe if we could prove Alex murdered her, then the courts would find his parents to not be appropriate to raise her.

I knew I was grasping at straws, but sometimes those straws led to answers.

I left Aunt Carrie and went up to my apartment to try and get some work done.

I looked at my calendar and saw that I had several clients scattered about in the coming few days, but didn't have anything that day.

Just when I decided that I probably needed an AA meeting, my phone vibrated. I looked and saw it was Amy.

"Hi, Amy, I'm so glad you called me back."

"You said it was urgent, but I don't know who this is."

"I know. Would you be able to meet me today sometime?"

"Who is this?"

"Oh, I'm sorry. My name is MJ Lange. I'm a psychologist and I'm trying to find some information for Carrie Pedersen concerning her daughter April. I believe you were friends with April and Alex, is that correct?"

I thought she had hung up on me because there was complete silence.

"Hello?"

"I'm still here. What could I possibly help you with? I haven't seen April for over a year."

"Please, could you just meet with me? Please."

"Okay, but I don't know how I'd be able to help you. It would be a waste of your time."

"Maybe, but I have nowhere else to go, and no one else to call."

We made a plan to meet early in the evening at a coffee shop in Venice near the Venice Pier. Probably nothing would pan out, but I needed to do something.

Until then, I had nothing to do, so I went to a badly needed AA meeting. I congratulated myself that I hadn't yet taken a drink, and I hadn't thought of Jesse the entire day.

Chapter 32

When I got to the coffee shop we had agreed upon, I knew immediately who Amy was. She looked almost exactly like April. Alex definitely had a type.

I ordered an iced tea and went and sat down across from her.

"I'm MJ, Amy; nice to meet you."

She fidgeted with her coffee cup and kept looking around like she expected to see someone, or something she didn't want to see.

"Are you okay?"

"Why are we here? What is it you need to know?"

"Are you aware that April was murdered?"

She gasped and brought her hand up to her mouth and looked straight into my eyes. Either she didn't know April was killed, or she was a very good actress.

"What happened?"

"She was strangled with some kind of a belt in her backyard. She had opened the door and gone out into her backyard in the evening, so they think she knew the person."

"Was it Alex?"

"Why would you say that?"

"Look, I was friends with both of them, but Alex was a bit much. He had April on a very tight leash, if you know what I mean. I didn't care much for him, but if April and I wanted to get together, he had to come along."

"So, you haven't gotten together with them for over a year?"

"That's right. Ever since April threw him out, we lost touch. I think she probably thought I was still in touch with him, but I wasn't. I decided that any kind of friendship with either one of them wouldn't work for me."

"Why was that?"

"Truth? Too much drama."

"Do you know anyone who may still be in touch with Alex, or have you heard if he has a new girlfriend since April threw him out?"

"I have no idea who might be in touch with him. I didn't know his friends, but I did run into him a couple of times, the last time about a month ago. We chatted a bit. He was bitter about April. Wanted to teach her a lesson, so was going after the kid. I told him that he sucked. He took that as a challenge and came on to me. I doubt he had another girlfriend. I think he would have bragged about it to me if he did."

"Why would he do that?"

She looked at me and said, "You don't know Alex, do you? If you did you'd know that he would be telling everyone who would listen that he had a new hot chick and to 'fuck April.' No, I doubt he was dating anyone, at least not seriously. He was too hung up on April and wanting to destroy her for ending it. What a creep."

I thanked her for her honesty and asked her to call me if she found out anything different about his dating or if she remembered that she knew someone who would still be in touch with him. I also told her to call the police if he tried to get a hold of her. She hadn't known he was missing and acted surprised.

As I was about to leave, I just had to ask, "Do you think Alex had it in him to strangle April? In cold blood? I mean, not because he got triggered and lost his temper, but could he have planned and executed a perfect murder, do you think?"

She scoffed and said, "Alex was a bully and bullies are chickenshits. He liked to manipulate and watch people squirm. If he killed her, it would take away his fun. Besides, he's sloppy; he would have left clues."

"I'm wondering why you remained friends with them if he was so awful?"

"I liked April. We had a lot in common. Alex wasn't so bad in the beginning, but as April and I became closer, he started acting possessive, so I basically put up with him. He treated me okay, but I saw how he treated April. The few times we were able to get together without Alex, I really enjoyed her wit and candor. I'm sorry she died. I really am."

After leaving Amy, I was once again struck how often people said they disliked Alex, but they didn't think he would murder anyone. They seemed to agree that he was more likely to torture them emotionally and play with them in order to prove that he was in control.

So, if he didn't kill April, who did? And, why did he disappear?

This question kept coming up over and over again, and it needed an answer. I dreaded going to my lonely apartment, especially since it was heating up from the hot days and it was very uncomfortable to be there in the evenings. There didn't seem to be any respite from the heat wave, just like there didn't seem to be any answers as to who killed April, and where Alex disappeared to.

I turned on the radio to distract me from my nagging thoughts. My mind drifted as I watched pedestrians enjoying the balmy evening weather, when it hit me. Could it be that he was also murdered and lying in some hole in the ground out in the desert? Should the police be looking at who had a motive to kill Alex? It would make sense that he was also killed.

I called Jesse to run this by him. When he answered and heard that I had some new theory, he asked me to meet him in person. Since I was almost home, I told him to meet me there. He said he'd be there in fifteen minutes.

When I heard him running up the stairs to my apartment, I went to open the door for him before he could knock.

He looked tired, and I asked if he'd eaten anything that day. When he told me he couldn't remember, I had him sit at my tiny little two-person table and made him a peanut butter sandwich with strawberry jam and found an old Diet Coke in the back of my small apartment refrigerator.

He ate the sandwich in about three bites, so I made him another one.

After he finished he looked at me and said, "Those were the best peanut butter and jelly sandwiches I have ever had. It hit the spot."

His smile was broad and it warmed my heart. I really had it bad for Jesse, but quickly hid it and started to tell him my new theory.

"Okay, let me get this straight. You now think that Alex did not kill April. That someone else did, set Alex up, and then did away with Alex?"

When he rephrased it that way, it did sound a bit out there and I frowned, because I hadn't really thought that if someone was setting Alex up for the murder, wouldn't they have left something of his for evidence?

We sat there staring at each other for a while until I broke the silence, "Look, Jesse, Alex has really totally disappeared. How could that be so? There's no evidence at the scene of April's murder to point to anyone. April knew the person because she opened the door and went outside. But she did lock the door behind her. Why?"

"To protect Joey."

"That's right. Who would she have to protect Joey from?"

"Not Alex because he already had part custody of her and she had given Joey to him as ordered by the court. So, if not Alex, then who?"

"We need to look into Estelle and Benjamin, Jesse."

"You think Estelle killed April and then got rid of her own son?"

"I don't know, but there is something all of us are missing."

"Motivation?"

"That's it. Motivation. Why would Estelle want Joey so badly? She didn't give a care about her for these past four years. Why now?"

"That's a good question. Let me look into it. I'm guessing it has something to do with all of her money. But to kill your own son? That's a bit much for me to accept."

I reminded him that most murders happened by people close to them, the ones that were supposed to love the victims the most.

"Yeah, you're right. But I could never see any scenario where I'd be willing to kill one of my sons. I don't think there would be any amount of money that could get me to do that. What else could be that strong of a motivation?"

I had no idea. And I wasn't even sure we were on the right track, but it did seem strange that all at once Estelle was interested in Joey, right after April was killed and Alex disappeared. There would be no one left to get in her way. She knew she could get Joey away from her other grandmother using her influence and her lawyers. That would have been a small inconvenience. However, getting Joey away from April and Alex would have been more difficult, if not impossible.

"Jesse, the real question here is why does Estelle want Joey so badly? You said you could look into that. How are you going to do that?"

He looked at me and told me that I didn't really need to know. I knew there was an issue in his past where he did something illegal in order to get a really bad guy locked up.

"Jesse, don't do anything that's going to come back on you. Promise me you won't do anything illegal. I couldn't live with myself if that happened."

"You don't have to worry about me doing anything illegal, but I have a few favors that I can call in and I think this is the time to do it."

After he left, I sat and worried. A little girl's life was at stake. If Jesse could gather information that could bring her back to her nana, then I wasn't going to ask how he did it.

Chapter 33

The next day, I had a couple clients in the morning, so I gave Aunt Carrie a call to let her know, but that I'd be free the rest of the day. I also asked her if Peter was able to find a way to bring Joey back yet.

I could imagine her sad face and slumped shoulders as she said, "Peter hasn't been able to quickly reverse the custody, but he does have the case on the docket."

"You mean, he's taking it to court?"

"Yes."

"When will that happen?"

"Not for three months."

I could hear the defeat in her voice. I knew the courts dragged their feet. I wasn't sure if they did it on purpose, or if things just took that long. You'd think they'd hire more people in order to get issues taken care of in a timely manner.

"We can't let Joey stay with Estelle for that long." I was trying to keep my voice calm, but even I could hear the anxiety in it. For a child three months would seem like an eternity.

"Peter told me to be patient. He has a few other things he is working on, but he suspects there is something more going on behind the scenes. Like maybe Estelle and Benjamin were bribing some key people in order to get them on their side. Or possibly they were calling in some favors? And before you say anything, MJ, no, there is no proof."

"If they are bribing the social workers or judges, then what good will it do if we go before the court?" I was so frustrated, I wanted to scream.

"Peter's trying to manipulate it so we have a judge that Peter trusts. I have no idea how all that works, or if he can even get that done without being accused of tampering."

I wanted so badly to tell her about what Jesse was up to, but decided that it wasn't fair to get her hopes up. I also didn't want her negativity and despair to affect my enthusiasm for getting Joey back, so I told her to hang in there and I'd see her later.

After seeing my clients, I sat and wrote up my notes. Feeling hungry, I scanned my almost bare refrigerator for something other than peanut butter. Finding some leftover Thai from my favorite Thai Bistro, I opened the container and gave it the smell test. The only smell was garlic, so I popped it in the microwave.

Before the microwave dinged, my phone vibrated in my pocket and saw it was Jesse. If he had some news already, he sure worked fast.

"Hi, Jesse."

"MJ, I got a hit already. You'll never guess what I found out."

"Stop playing with me and tell."

"Estelle? She's sick. She has ovarian cancer. That's why she's so skinny. She doesn't have long to live."

I couldn't believe my ears. She's sick with cancer? What would that mean? If she was dying, then why go to great lengths to get Joey? She wouldn't even be able to take care of her physically, but then again, she'd have enough money to hire it done.

"Jesse, I don't understand. What does this mean?"

"I'm not sure, but this information is important enough that I need to tell the detectives who are working on this case."

"Of course you do." Maybe this was the break we needed. Maybe the fact that she doesn't have long to live is why she did her best to make sure Joey would come and live with her now. She didn't have time to waste on letting the courts decide and then having to wait longer if Aunt Carrie won and she had to contest the decision. She couldn't take any chances, so she had to make sure she got Joey immediately."

Jesse then went on to wonder out loud if we misjudged Estelle and that her only wish was to spend her last dying days with a granddaughter she had rebuffed in the past and wanted to make it up to her.

It made sense that Estelle had cancer since I had already thought that may be the case. I still didn't see why she had to get legal custody over Joey though. If she wanted to spend time with her as a last dying wish, all she had to do was talk to Aunt Carrie. She would have gladly worked with her to allow Estelle to spend time with her. None of what Estelle was doing was making any sense.

"I need to tell Aunt Carrie this. She needs to let Peter know this information so there can be some kind of emergency intervention. I think Aunt Carrie would be compassionate enough to allow Estelle to spend time with Joey if that's what's actually happening."

"Let's not jump to conclusions just yet. There's more investigating to be done and we don't want to spill the beans about everything we are learning just yet, in case there is something more sinister going on."

He did agree with me that Aunt Carrie and Peter should be told the news, and then he told me that he was going to follow that particular thread to see where it led.

With the HIPAA confidentiality laws in place, I did not want to know how Jesse got this information about Estelle's cancer, so I didn't ask.

After calling Aunt Carrie and telling her what Jesse had found out, she said, "Oh my, that's why she needed to get Joey so quickly. That makes perfect sense. I'll let Peter know. Maybe he can arrange some kind of shared custody until she passes."

That's why I loved Aunt Carrie. She always understood what the other person was feeling and why people can act so badly. She put herself in their shoes. Me, I wanted Peter to throw the book at Estelle for not being honest, but mainly for scaring our vulnerable Joey.

I was beginning to think of Joey as 'ours,' not mine and not Aunt Carrie's, but 'ours.' There was nothing I wouldn't do for Joey. She was family and I was going to make sure she got all the love she deserved.

If Peter could arrange some kind of agreement with Estelle and Benjamin, I would go for it, because at least Joey would be with us half of the time. Half time was better than no time.

I began to feel a little better, that there might be a solution. The fact that Estelle had cancer and was dying meant we found the reason why she was so eager to quickly take charge of Joey. That mystery was solved. But it still didn't solve who killed April nor tell us where Alex was. And I wasn't sure I trusted Estelle, even if she was dying from cancer. Maybe I needed to go talk to her. Just the two of us to see what she was really thinking.

With that plan of action, I got her contact information from Aunt Carrie, who immediately cautioned me to not make matters worse. She didn't think it was a good idea for me to talk to Estelle and wanted us to let the lawyer deal with it.

I didn't disagree with her, but I also needed to have a one-on-one with Estelle for my peace of mind. I may have misjudged her and if I was to stop worrying about Joey, I needed to know what was in her heart.

She agreed to meet me at a cozy little restaurant in Santa Monica. It was tucked away from the busy streets and no one would even know it was there unless someone told you about it. There wasn't even a sign with the name of it on the building and I wasn't even sure the door I went into was the right one.

Estelle had a private table overlooking a garden in the back and the hostess graciously showed me to it.

I wasn't really dressed for such an elegant place and felt a bit uncomfortable, until I remembered that I was there to find out more about Estelle. I wasn't there to impress anyone.

She indicated for me to sit down and asked if I'd like something to drink. I could see that she had a martini half drunk sitting in front of her. Sitting in the cozy comfortable chair, surrounded by a beautiful garden, soft music playing and a light cool breeze ruffling my hair, I so wanted an ice cold martini.

But I declined and asked for an iced tea instead. I wasn't there socially, or to have lunch, but to have a chat with Estelle.

We sat in silence until Estelle finally asked, "So, Ms. Lange, what is it you needed to see me about?"

"I think you know."

"What about Joey?"

"Why now? You haven't even so much as sent her a card for her birthday, so why now?"

She took a moment to pluck her olive out of her martini glass with her long bony fingers and chewed on it as she took another sip of her drink before answering. "Alex and I have been estranged, as you probably know. As long as he was around her, I wasn't able to really carry out my duties as a grandmother because Alex wouldn't have allowed it. Since he has disappeared, this is a good time for me to connect with her."

I wanted to tell her that her answer was bullshit. There were a lot of ways for her to connect with Joey without getting legal custody of her, but I said, instead, "You know how close Joey is to Carrie. Taking her from her beloved grandmother right after she lost her mother was cruel."

"Maybe so, but I had to act quickly."

"Why?"

"You have no idea what's at stake here and I'm not in a position to explain it to you. Just know that Joey living with me will ultimately be the best for her. I can assure you, she'll have an enviable life."

"You mean because of all your money, right?"

"It's more than money, Ms. Lange. Surely you wouldn't want to deprive her of her birthright. She will be the heiress of billions. She can be, have, and do whatever she wants. But she has to be brought up a certain way, or she'll just squander it if she hasn't been properly prepared."

I realized that Estelle actually believed what she was saying. She didn't even mention love. It all had to do with money and prestige and I didn't know how to counter with something that she could understand. I did the best I could by saying, "You are discounting the deep love and connection between Joey and her grandmother. I see that you haven't even taken that into consideration."

"Oh, Ms. Lange, don't be so dramatic. She'll learn to love what I have to offer."

I had a difficult time understanding how she could be so cold and stared at her until I remembered her cancer and said, "I hear you're dying of cancer. Is this why you've acted so quickly in getting Joey into your custody?"

"And what if it is?"

"If that is the case, then I know Carrie would be more than willing to share custody with you, so you could get to know Joey and spend as much time as you'd like with her before you pass."

A brief shadow passed over her face and for a moment I thought I saw something deeper inside of her—maybe regrets, disappointments. Maybe she, herself was robbed of her own childhood the same way she was going to be robbing Joey of hers. But just as quickly as that peek of humanity appeared on her face, she immediately withdrew it as she threw her head back and laughed, saying, "Oh, Ms. Lange, you are naive. It tickles me that you're so childishly innocent that you'd think I'd actually consider something like that. Why should I? I have the legal documents. I don't need to compromise, do I?"

I looked at her pale face and faded blue eyes and saw only malice. When she picked up her martini, all I could see were huge diamonds and whatever other expensive stones she had sparkling and glittering on her bony fingers.

All I felt was pity for her. I doubted that she had any real friends and what I saw between her and Benjamin wasn't something I'd care to have with a spouse. I came away from that meeting feeling that she was lonely. A lonely woman with more money than she knew what to do with. I was lonely too, but didn't feel like I could reach out to her with that truth. No, Estelle Spark would never admit that kind of vulnerability, but I felt it, and I knew that as much money as she had, she'd never be able to buy her way out of that loneliness.

I still didn't see her motivation for trying to gain Joey's custody, but maybe I just didn't have all of the facts.

Chapter 34

After my meeting with Estelle, I found myself void of any pressing action I needed to take to get Joey back. I allowed myself to take a long walk. I put on my walking shoes and sprang down the steps and out the door where I literally almost ran into Abe Larson. It looked like he was on his way to my place, clipboard in hand, pen behind his ear.

"MJ, just the person I was looking for. I need you to do a walk-through to sign off on the painting. That and a few minor things and it is completely done. You should be able to move into your house by next week."

Instead of elation and joy, Abe saw my face fall and I immediately tried a smile and forced cheerfulness into my voice and said, "That's great, Abe."

He didn't buy it, but asked, instead, if I could do the walk-through right then and there.

I hesitated because I was so looking forward to my walk, but knew that I was just trying to put it off. I was still ambivalent about living in the house where I had to defend myself. Maybe I had more work to do on that particular trauma.

I agreed and followed him into the back porch, a porch that could be walled in with glass or opened all the way up as if it was part of the soon-to-be-garden. It was my favorite room in the whole remodel. It had also been the office room where Detective Slatter, aka Mike Rimichi, tried to strangle me.

He tried to strangle me, just like April was strangled. Except April was strangled with a belt and Rimichi had used his arm to snuff the life out of me. No wonder I was kind of losing it ever since April was found murdered. I hadn't consciously put the two events together yet, because April died and I didn't.

I started to shake and understood exactly what April had felt. If it wasn't for a client who had been stalking me breaking into my office window and distracting Rimichi, I would be dead.

The thought shook me. I never actually felt the horror of almost dying.

April had no one stalking her to come to her rescue. She knew she was dying. She probably cried out for her mother and felt the sorrow of leaving her little girl behind.

I couldn't stop shaking and Abe, who had continued on into the rest of the house, finally realized I wasn't following him. He came back with a worried look on his face and quickly had me lie on the floor putting my knees up, thinking I was going into shock.

I don't know where he found it, but he had a blanket that he placed over me and I heard him call an ambulance. I tried to tell him not to call, that I was okay, but I couldn't make my teeth stop chattering.

I was definitely having a PTSD panic reaction, but didn't know how to stop it.

The next thing I knew, Aunt Carrie was kneeling beside me with a cup of hot tea with tons of sugar in it and making me take small sips as she held my head up.

"What I really wanted to give you was a shot of whiskey, but I knew you were coming up on your fourth month of sobriety, so didn't want to spoil it for you."

I slowly sat up as the paramedics came storming into my brand new home. They quickly assessed the situation, took my vitals, and then pronounced me good to go. They suggested that I go to bed and drink plenty of fluids. They assumed with the hot weather that I had gotten dehydrated, saying this was their fourth call of the day for dehydration.

Abe and Aunt Carrie helped me up and feeling only slightly woozy, I insisted that we continue the walk-through, as long as Aunt Carrie would agree to do it with me.

The colors were muted and the openness of the house allowed the hot sun to blaze in. Since it was a hot day, we all felt the heat, but Abe then showed me how to use the A/C and I was glad that I had decided to spend the extra money for a good top of the line central heat and air.

I didn't know why I had been so reluctant to embrace the newly rebuilt home, because with Aunt Carrie by my side, it felt perfect. I could and would move into it, starting next week.

Later, after Abe left, Aunt Carrie said, "Okay, MJ, what was that all about? Dehydration? I don't think so."

I agreed to make an extra appointment with my trauma therapist and wondered if I'd ever really be okay again. I didn't tell Aunt Carrie that my PTSD came from my imagining, or my actually knowing, how April had felt at the end. I just couldn't do that to her. She didn't need to know that.

I never did get that walk but was glad Aunt Carrie was sitting with me as we enjoyed the open porch in my new home. Just then I felt my phone vibrate. Thinking it was Jesse again, I quickly plucked it out of my pocket and said, "What now?"

Instead of Jesse, I heard Nancy Friday's loud voice booming through the phone and I quickly put her on audio so we could both hear her.

"Slow down, Nancy. I have you on speaker because Carrie Pedersen is here with me. What's going on? Is Jimmy okay?"

"That's why I'm calling you. We've already called the police, but I wanted you to also know what happened."

Aunt Carrie and I looked at each other and I shrugged my shoulders because I couldn't imagine why they'd have to call the cops.

"Jimmy was fooling around with my phone earlier and he started to look at photos. I have tons of photos and videos of him growing up and he enjoys them."

I knew it might take Nancy a long time to get to the point, but I didn't want to stop her or she'd go onto a different tangent, so I just said, "Go on, we're listening."

"Well, he found some videos of when he was a baby and started watching them. I didn't think anything of it, to tell the truth."

"Nancy, did he find something that pertains to April?"

I couldn't allow her to continue in her chatty way of talking. I was too anxious. I suspected Jimmy had found something.

"Keep your pants on, I'm coming to it. Well, he started to look at more recent photos and he opened up the video I had taken at April's memorial. You know, when Joey's other grandparents came to grab her?"

"Yes?" I tried not to interrupt again but I could hardly hold it in. I glanced at Aunt Carrie and she was leaning forward in order to hear every word.

"Well, when he saw the grandpa, he started yelling."

"Benjamin?"

"If that's the guy's name, then yes, Benjamin. Anyway, I came running to see what got Jimmy so excited. He kept pointing at the guy and yelling, 'That's him. That's him'"

Jimmy recognized Benjamin. He hadn't been at the memorial, so he hadn't seen Benjamin come in with Estelle, but he'd seen him somewhere, most likely at April's house.

"Did Jimmy tell you where he saw Benjamin? Was it before April was murdered?"

"Yep. Jimmy said that the guy had come to visit April days before April died. For Jimmy, days could mean weeks, or months, so it's going to be hard to pinpoint, but I'm working on it."

"I'm coming over."

Aunt Carrie got up and told me she was coming with me, and I couldn't stop her.

Chapter 35

There was already a police car parked in front of Nancy's house when we got there. Aunt Carrie had called Detective Myer on our way, but when we entered the house, the detectives hadn't arrived yet.

Two policemen were standing inside the door with a look of confusion on their faces. Nancy was talking a mile a minute and I'm pretty sure she wasn't making any sense.

I introduced myself and told them that the detectives who were working on the case of April's murder were on their way; maybe we should wait for them to arrive so Jimmy wouldn't have to explain what he knew more than once.

They could see that Jimmy was socially awkward, so took pity on him and said it was a good idea to wait.

Jimmy and I had bonded when I had been at his house before. So while we waited, I asked him what he was working on, hoping to keep him from getting overly excited and losing focus.

Once Detective Myer and her partner Dunham got there, we all casually took our seats in the living room. Nancy excused herself to get us some refreshments from the kitchen. Aunt Carrie followed her, saying she probably needed some help. But I knew that Aunt Carrie followed her so she'd be out of our way when the detectives asked Jimmy questions about what he had seen. Nancy had a way of inserting herself that wasn't useful.

Aunt Carrie had informed them on the phone as to what had happened when Jimmy saw the video, so they were already a step ahead.

The patrol men were let go, but asked to write a report about what they had witnessed. I was glad. The fewer people around, the safer Jimmy would feel.

With Nancy and Aunt Carrie out of the way, they allowed me to stay with Jimmy. He backed away from Detective Dunham and was more receptive to Myer, but kept looking at me.

I took the initiative and asked, "Jimmy, you saw a video on your mom's phone a little bit ago. Can you tell us what you saw?"

He didn't look at either of the detectives and kept his focus on me, although he didn't actually make eye contact. He moved closer to me, but we did not touch and I kept my hands to myself, even though I wanted to put my arm around him and tell him everything was going to be all right.

"It was that guy."

"What guy was that, Jimmy?" Detective Myer asked. I had to give Detective Dunham kudos for staying back and allowing us to question Jimmy.

"The guy who made April cry."

"When did he make April cry?" This was from me.

He couldn't answer that question, so I asked him if it happened when he was still in school.

"No, I was out of school for summer vacation. It was the week Mama took me to get my hair cut."

That information gave us a potential time frame. We could ask his mother when she took him to get his hair cut. I was almost positive Nancy would be able to give us the exact date and time.

Detective Myer took over, "Jimmy, this is really important and we are so glad you recognized this man. Do you know why he made April cry?"

Jimmy looked away and started tapping his foot.

I crossed my fingers in hopes that his mother didn't come rushing back into the room and get him distracted by telling her own version of what happened.

"Jimmy, did you hear what this guy said to April?"

He looked toward me and said, "I don't like that guy. I wanted him to leave."

"Did he stay long?"

He just shrugged his shoulders.

"Did you ever see him come back?"

He shrugged his shoulders again.

I realized that was probably the most we were going to get out of Jimmy, but it was a clue.

Detective Myer tried again with a few more questions, but Jimmy clammed up and continued to tell us that he didn't like the guy.

After Nancy was asked to call them if Jimmy remembered anything else, we all left Nancy and Jimmy alone to eat the refreshments Nancy had brought out. We all politely took a cookie and Aunt Carrie thanked Nancy for her trouble.

Nancy had been able to tell us exactly when Jimmy had his hair appointment, so we could narrow down the time Benjamin visited April to the week it happened. It had been just a couple of weeks before she was murdered.

After leaving Jimmy's house, we stood together in a huddle in front of Detective Myer's unmarked car. Since I was the one that made it safe for Jimmy to disclose what he knew, I guess they felt it was okay for them to discuss the implication of Benjamin being at April's house just weeks before she was murdered.

"Let's not start thinking the worst here." Detective Dunham said, "He may have come to let April know Estelle was dying and if she had it in her heart to let them spend some time with Joey."

"Why would that make April cry? She wasn't close to Estelle and in fact Estelle was quite cool to her and rejected her grandchild, Joey. That couldn't have made April feel much sorrow for her."

I looked at Aunt Carrie for her to confirm my statement and saw that she was nodding her head in agreement. She had seemed lost in thought and not much engaged in our discussion.

"Maybe he was threatening her. She may have refused to allow them to see her daughter because they had done such a rotten job with their son, Alex, that she didn't want them anywhere near Joey."

That seemed to get Aunt Carrie's attention and she said, "Yes, that would make sense because my April was very protective of Joey."

"Aunt Carrie, did April tell you that Benjamin came to see her?"

"No, she didn't. She was protective of me also. She probably didn't want to worry me unnecessarily. I hope that if she had really felt threatened she would have come to me about it. It breaks my heart to think that she was all alone with her fears."

Detective Myer, who had been very quiet, told us that there was no point in speculating. She thought the best course of action was for her and her partner to go have a talk with the Sparks.

"Any chance we could come along with you?" I asked, ever hopeful, knowing that we might be able to see Joey.

"No, ma'am. We know what we're doing. This is new information that we need to look into. However, it could be very innocent and nothing may come of it."

I was disappointed. I thought it was very important information, and was the first real break we had. Too bad Jimmy wasn't able to tell us more of what Benjamin said. I thought I might circle back in a day or two and talk to Jimmy again one-on-one. I thought with just the two of us, he might be able to talk about it, or remember what April and Benjamin had been talking about.

I drove Aunt Carrie home in silence. When we arrived, I turned to her and asked if she was okay. I asked if she wanted me to come and stay with her,

"I'm tired, MJ. I'm going to go in and take a nap."

I reached over and patted her arm and reassured her that I'd be close by, just like she was close by when I had my PTSD attack earlier. I told her I loved her and that I wasn't giving up on getting Joey back.

I didn't tell her that I was also never going to give up on finding out who murdered April. I didn't think I could rest until that murder was solved, but I had no idea what the next step should be.

Chapter 36

I couldn't wait to call Jesse and let him know what Jimmy had said. Surely, Jesse would have an opinion about it. I did not think for a minute that Benjamin showing up at April's house was innocent.

It concerned me that it was Benjamin who had appeared at April's house. He was the good grandparent, wasn't he? I had told Joey to trust him. I wasn't so sure anymore. Estelle was dying, she had a reason for seeking Joey out. Once she was gone, Benjamin could make his own decisions around his granddaughter. He wouldn't need Estelle's permission anymore. He might even make amends with his son Alex, if Alex ever appeared again.

Was that Benjamin's end game here, to get Joey in order for Alex to get her back? Was he threatening April that they were going to get custody of Joey for their son Alex? That would have upset April.

I left a message for Jesse to call me back and sat down waiting for his call. I sat on my sofa that looked out over my brand new house to the ocean. I could tell that the sunset was going to be spectacular because there were clouds streaking toward the horizon and I saw there was already a bit of orange color in them.

I was so grateful for the view and wished I had someone to share it with. I contemplated going to get Aunt Carrie, but she did look exhausted and needed to sleep.

Instead of calling me, maybe Jesse would just come over. We could watch the sunset together and then talk about what Jimmy said.

I shook my head in disgust, reminding myself that he was married. I was playing with fire even allowing him to help us in our quest for justice. But he did find out that Estelle was dying of cancer. That was an important piece of information and if he was following that lead, who knows what he might be able to find.

Jesse was a good detective and I wondered why he wasn't one. Why was he still a patrol officer? He had come to see me professionally over a year ago because he had been in trouble at work. He was forced to go into therapy due to some anger issues.

What his superiors didn't know, and what he did confidentially disclose to me in therapy, was that he had planted some evidence on a dirty criminal. However, the criminal had gotten off because his politician father had made a deal for him, or paid someone off.

Jesse had been furious because the guy had been part of a sex trade organization, if not *the* head of it. He planted the evidence because he felt that it was the right thing to do to put this guy out of commission. We had gone round and round about this. Me, calling Jesse a vigilante and Jesse defending his position in order to save those young girls. He used the argument that vigilantes were citizens taking matters into their own hands without legal authority and since he was part of the legal authority, he wasn't a vigilante.

I could see his passion and his need to rescue those girls and I had to agree that the sex trade had to be brought to its knees, but that it had to be done under the rule of law and since Jesse was part of the justice system, it was even worse for him to have done what he did.

I did have to admit to myself that I emotionally agreed with him on what he did, even though logically I had to oppose his actions.

The problem with what he did was that he hadn't been able to completely hide his actions and another client of mine had found out what he had done and had blackmailed him.

It was the client who had been stalking me, and was still in a psychiatric hospital with a poor prognosis. There is still a strong possibility that this client will get better and either try to blackmail Jesse again, or inform on him.

Jesse and I never talked about that client. For him it was 'out of sight, out of mind.' But I knew enough as a psychotherapist that denial isn't always the best way to go.

I felt my phone vibrate. It was Jesse.

"Hey, MJ," he said before I had a chance to answer. "What's up?"

"Something happened today that might be significant. I'd really like to hear what you think about it."

After I told him about Jimmy, he asked if he could come over so we could talk about it more in detail. Plus, he told me that he may have some interesting information for me too by the time he got to my place.

I hesitated for only a nanosecond. The colors of the sunset were turning the inside of my apartment a golden hue that gave it a feeling of warmth and coziness. I wanted Jesse to come over.

As I opened the door for Jesse, I could see the beautiful sunset—a deep blood-orange with streaks of purple. My apartment was filled with the golden warmth of the setting sun. It felt other-worldly.

We stared at each other for a moment and then simultaneously reached out. We embraced and stood together as warmth and colors surrounded us.

We stayed that way and I felt as if we were in an alternate universe. The sun set, giving my apartment a feeling of emptiness. We stepped away from each other and both of us looked down, unable to meet each other's eyes. I was embarrassed for showing my intense feelings toward him. I didn't know what Jesse was feeling.

We awkwardly sat on the sofa and watched the rest of the sunset until it grew dark outside and I got up to turn on some lights.

Neither one of us mentioned the heat between us. It was a boundary we had both stepped across and I wasn't sure we could put it back.

"You go first," I finally said. I wanted to know what he thought about Jimmy having seen Benjamin Spark at April's a couple of weeks before her murder. And I especially wanted to know what he thought about Benjamin making April cry.

He drew his hand over his face and let out a long sigh. "I honestly don't know what to make of it. It could be a lot of different things. Since neither one of them had been in contact with April since the birth of Joey, I'm surprised April didn't share this with her mother."

"Yeah, me too. It could have been something very innocent, like him sharing Estelle's cancer with April and maybe pleading with her to allow them to see their granddaughter. But why would that be a secret? Seems like that would be something April would share with her mother. Or, maybe she just hadn't gotten around to it yet?"

Jesse appeared thoughtful, as he squinted his eyes and nodded his head in agreement.

I added, "I've been going on the assumption that Estelle swooped in and took advantage of the situation when April was murdered and Alex disappeared. Maybe there's more to this. Maybe there is a connection."

"You think they killed April and then disappeared their son?"

"Before I knew Estelle had cancer and got to know her a bit, I could have seen her doing something like that, but she seems too frail to pull it off now. And I can't imagine Benjamin murdering April and then killing his own son. Benjamin seems more like a coward who just goes along with Estelle. I couldn't see him having the courage or malice to do anything like that."

"There has to be more to this entire story, MJ. We just don't have all the facts. I thought I was going to have some new information by the time I got here tonight, but I haven't received anything yet."

When I asked him what he thought he was going to get, he told me he was working on an angle having to do with Estelle's will. Since she knew she was dying very soon, she may have decided to change some things around before it was too late. Maybe there was something in there that someone didn't like. Maybe she was giving a large chunk of her money to April and then someone who thought they were inheriting it got greedy and got rid of her.

"You mean like Alex or Benjamin? Jesse, we have to find a way to see what's in her will," I said.

"MJ, this is just a thought I had. It doesn't mean that it's true. I don't have a way to get a hold of her will, do you?"

Of course, I had no idea how one would be able to see someone's will. There had to be another way to find out what was in it. Besides, if she did change it, would she have told the people who thought they were inheriting? If she hadn't told, then there wouldn't be a motivation to kill April. And how would we know if she told or not?

Just then, Jesse's phone went off and when he saw who was calling, he stepped away from me and turned his back. I couldn't really hear what he was saying, but when he turned around after the end of the call, he had a big grin on his face.

"What?"

Chapter 37

"You'll never guess."

"Just tell me already, Jesse." I was on pins and needles and wasn't in the mood to be teased.

"Alex isn't Benjamin's biological son."

"What?"

"Yeah, Benjamin and Estelle got married when Alex was eight. Benjamin adopted Alex when Alex was ten."

"So, where is the biological father? Is he still around? And whose money is it, anyway?" Even though I couldn't picture Benjamin as a tough businessman, I had originally assumed he had made his money in the stock market, or in something that paid off big. I figured he was probably some kind of genius who knew how to make money using his brains.

Jesse looked at me and said, "It's from the Spark family. It's old money and there's a lot of it. Estelle was the only grandchild of the late Alfred Spark, who made all that money. In my research, I found that in order for the family name to carry on, anyone who married her would have had to take her surname. My source told me that is exactly what Benjamin did. He took Estelle's name. His last name is actually Hamilton.

I guessed having a boy was a big deal for Estelle, but he must have done something really bad to have had her disown him, since he would have been the last male to carry on the Spark name.

"Jesse, can you find out more about Alex? Does he have a record? Why would Estelle disown him?"

"I'm on it. I'll do it first thing in the morning, but I really have to get going now."

I understood. He needed to be home with his family. He wasn't wearing his uniform, so I guessed he was off duty. I wondered what he was going to tell his wife about where he was and I properly felt guilty.

As I walked Jesse to the door, he turned and I felt that he was about to embrace me again, so I put my hand out and whispered, "What happened earlier tonight can never happen again. You know that, right?"

He backed away like he had been slapped and abruptly turned and left, taking the stairs down two at a time.

It was difficult watching him run down the steps and I had an urge to call him back, but knew I shouldn't. If Big Al had seen us embracing in the glow of the sunset, he would have been very disappointed in me.

I was disappointed in me. I knew part of me was using the fact that Jesse was helping us get Joey back as an excuse to see him, be near him.

Damn, I had been such an idiot. But I did have more information than I had at the beginning of the day, so he was being really helpful. Actually, he seemed to be doing more than the detectives on the case.

I knew that Benjamin had seen April a few weeks before she was murdered and said something to her that made her cry. I knew that Alex wasn't Benjamin's biological son. And I knew that the Spark wealth was from Estelle, not Benjamin.

My gut was telling me that whatever it was, it had to do with the money. I didn't know how much they were worth, so I googled the family. I had never heard of the Spark family but the internet did not disappoint. Apparently Estelle's grandfather had made his money from the stock market and then successfully invested in real estate. Estelle was worth well over 20 billion dollars.

I was impressed because that was a lot of money. Enough to kill for.

I texted this amount to Jesse and asked him if he had given his information about Alex being adopted by Benjamin to Detective Myer. I wasn't sure if they had already interviewed Benjamin in order to follow up on why he was at April's house and what it was that he said to her that made her cry, but the fact that Alex wasn't his biological son was new information they needed to know.

I called Aunt Carrie to find out if the detectives had gotten back to her after interviewing the Sparks, or if she had heard anything regarding Benjamin's visit to April.

After letting the call go to her voicemail, I looked at the time and suspected she might already be asleep and I didn't want to disturb her. This would all have to wait until morning.

I'm not a very patient person. As a psychotherapist, I appear calm and patient on the outside, but I am often antsy on the inside. I know where it is my clients need to go way before they understand it themselves and I get impatient waiting for them to catch up.

My trauma therapist and I had been working on me doing more meditating and using relaxation exercises along with deep breathing, so I decided to sit in my yoga position on the floor and practice.

However, my mind just kept going over and over the facts as we knew them about the Sparks, Joey, and April's murder. The biggest mystery to me was why Alex disappeared. It didn't make any sense.

I was also worried about Joey. After getting the information about Benjamin being at their house making April cry, I wasn't sure Joey was safe.

As I started counting my inhales and my exhales, I started to relax. My mind drifted again, but not to the murder. I was imagining my safe spot, which was in the Red Wood Groves in Northern California. I love those huge trees and whenever I am near them, I feel in awe of them, safe and secure.

Just as I was drifting off, all of a sudden I felt a flash go off in my brain. It felt almost like a lightning flash and I jerked awake. I was still sitting on the floor, but my body was slumped over. I must have fallen asleep and I looked around me feeling a little disoriented.

Something in my unconscious mind had been speaking to me right before the flash occurred and I sat still waiting for it to resurface.

As I sat in my yoga position on the floor, I remembered I was thinking about the puzzle of why Benjamin had visited April, right before I fell asleep. *What was it that was bothering me?*

And then I remembered. I had wondered if Joey was at home the day Benjamin came to April's home. She must not have been because she would have remembered him either at the funeral home, or at the memorial.

But maybe she did remember him. When the Sparks came walking up to us at the funeral home, Joey had shrunk against me in fear. I had thought she was afraid of Estelle's stern and cold demeanor, because that was what I had reacted to.

But what if it was Benjamin she was afraid of? What if she heard what he had said to her mother?

It was clear that I needed to see Joey. I needed to find out what it was she knew. She could be in danger if she overheard something that could implicate Benjamin.

I stood up quickly and was determined to call Jesse. I didn't care that it was almost midnight. This seemed too important to wait until the morning. Benjamin could be hurting Joey and she had no way to defend herself. I started to panic and couldn't find my phone.

As I hunted in vain, I stopped and forced myself to slow down. I needed to back off instead of going off half-cocked like I was prone to do. My impulsivity had gotten me in a lot of trouble in the past and I was working on thinking things through first.

I had no idea if Benjamin was a bad person or not. All we had on him was that he wasn't Alex's biological father, and he visited April who ended up crying. It didn't mean he made her cry. Maybe he said something that triggered her to cry.

When Estelle and Benjamin came to take Joey, she didn't seem scared of Benjamin then, so maybe Joey really was just scared of Estelle and she didn't hear what made her mother cry.

My mind wouldn't stop. I started to imagine other possibilities. Like, what if Estelle was leaving everything to Joey? What if she had cut Benjamin out of her will and she either told him that, or he got wind of it in some way?

We really needed to know what was in Estelle's will. If she was cutting Benjamin out of her will and giving all her money to Joey, would that have meant April would have been in charge of all that wealth as Joey's legal guardian? Killing April would then make sense. So the next logical step would be to eventually get rid of Joey, putting her in danger.

Maybe Benjamin was threatening April to not accept the inheritance, but I don't know if that's even possible. Can one say no to an inheritance for her daughter? I guess she could give all the money to Benjamin. Maybe he was using threats against Joey in order to assure April would give it to him.

It was getting late and I was getting a headache trying to figure it all out. I had to stop a minute and ask myself what my goal was.

It was to get Joey back living with her nana. It wasn't to figure out who murdered April, or where her father had hidden himself. But these new developments sure did seem important to me at three a.m.

Chapter 38

I must have drifted off finally, because I woke when I felt my phone vibrate. It was in my pocket and I saw that the caller was Aunt Carrie, just the person I wanted to talk to.

"Aunt Carrie, I need you to try and get us in to talk to Joey as quickly as possible."

"Well, good morning to you too, MJ. Of course, I'd love to talk to Joey, but so far, Peter hasn't had any luck getting that to happen."

"Aunt Carrie, I had an idea in the middle of the night and I need to check it out with Joey. I can't explain it all right this minute, but it's important. Can you give them a call, or ask Peter to arrange it now?"

"Okay, MJ, but I already told you that Peter hasn't been able to get me a visit yet, so I don't think it's going to happen any time soon. Why don't you come on over and we'll make a plan, or you can talk to Peter. I made chocolate chip pancakes."

"Joey's favorite," I said under my breath.

I knew she was compensating for the loss of Joey. She needed something to do that felt like she was still taking care of her little grandchild. I understood.

I quickly showered and threw on some bluejeans and a t-shirt. It felt cooler and I hoped the heat wave had come to an end.

When I stepped into Aunt Carrie's kitchen, the smell of cinnamon and vanilla was overpowering and I sat down to let her serve me her famous pancakes.

After we finished eating I asked her if she had tried again to set up a meeting with Joey.

"I left word for Peter, but he hasn't called me back yet. It's still early in the morning, MJ; give him a minute to respond."

I got up and went to pour myself another cup of her bitter coffee and unconsciously poured some cream into my cup. When I took a sip, I almost spit it out and looked to see why the coffee tasted so different.

"MJ, what's going on? Tell me what you've learned. I know you're on to something. I need to know. I need to know you aren't going to make a lot of wild accusations and cause more bad blood between Joey's other grandparents and me. Promise me you won't."

She knew me too well. Even though I used alcohol for decades to hide my low self-esteem and feelings of unworthiness, I still barged into things without pausing. I wanted to reassure her, but I wasn't sure I could with what I thought was at stake.

"All I'm trying to do is find out if Joey was in the house and heard what Benjamin said to April that upset her so much. I could even talk to Joey on the phone. Or, we could call the detectives and have them do the interview."

"MJ, I'm hoping Peter can create a plan where we can share Joey for now. Please don't make waves. I need that girl back where she belongs, if we start stepping on Estelle's toes, she'll pull the plug and won't cooperate. Please, please stay out of it."

I looked at Aunt Carrie and felt ashamed. It was her granddaughter. She had just lost a daughter and all I could think about is how much I wanted Joey back. I was already thinking of her as my little girl. Those kinds of thoughts were not good for me.

I started pacing around in her kitchen, feeling like I was in a prison. I wanted Peter to call back and tell us that he got the meeting.

After thirty minutes or so, I gave up. I couldn't stand it anymore. So much for patience. I hugged Aunt Carrie goodbye and told her not to worry, that I wasn't going to jeopardize her getting Joey back. I then headed out to find my car down the street.

I wasn't sure what my next step was, but then I remembered that I was going to go back to visit Jimmy when it was just him and me, and maybe Nancy. Surely, he'd be able to be more specific as to what Benjamin had said to April. If I couldn't get to Joey, then I'd try Jimmy.

It was difficult to comprehend that it was all coming down to a four-year-old and a young man who was on the spectrum.

I grabbed my phone and called Nancy. She answered with a bright good morning and asked how I was doing.

In order not to get her started with all of her chatter, I asked her if Jimmy was home and if so, could I come over and talk with him again.

"Sure, come right on over. Jimmy's here. We've got nothin' planned for today. Be nice to have some company."

When I arrived, I hadn't really planned on how I was going to talk to Jimmy, but I knew I didn't want to spook him, so I accepted Nancy's coffee and pastries, even though I was already full from Aunt Carrie's pancakes.

Jimmy came to the table soon after I sat down and helped himself to one of the pastries.

"Hey, Jimmy. How's it going?"

"Why are you here again?"

That was very direct. I thought we had made a nice connection, but his question threw me and I wasn't so sure he was glad to see me. I decided I'd be direct too.

"I came by to talk to you when the police aren't here. I thought they may have made you nervous and you may have forgotten some of the things you had seen or heard."

"You mean when that guy made April cry?"

"Yes, exactly. I was wondering if you could remember what it was that made April cry? Did he say something to her that made her sad?"

"She wasn't sad. She was crying because she was upset."

"Oh, okay. Do you know what she was upset about?"

Jimmy then did something interesting. He took on a deep voice as he parroted what Benjamin must have said to April, "You know I'm right.'"

He then started eating his pastry and asked his mother for a glass of milk, having returned to himself.

"Jimmy, did you hear anything else? Did April say anything?"

"That's when April got upset and started crying."

"Did she say anything, or did the guy you saw say anything else that you can remember?"

"April didn't say anything, she just sat at the table and cried."

"How about the guy?"

"The guy got up, pointed at her and said, 'I'm the only one who can protect you and Joey. Do the right thing.'"

Again, Jimmy mimicked a deep male voice.

After questioning Jimmy again to see if there was anything else, I finally gave up. Jimmy had said all he was going to say.

I looked at Nancy, who just shrugged, and said, "Thank you for letting me talk to Jimmy. He's a good kid."

As I left and got into my car, I was maybe more puzzled than when I first went in to talk to Jimmy. *What did it all mean?*

Chapter 39

As I drove back home, I went over in my head what Jimmy had heard. It didn't sound like Benjamin was threatening April, but maybe had information that was a threat to her. Maybe he was warning her instead. Maybe my initial reaction to him was correct and that he was to be trusted.

But who would be causing April and Joey harm? With Estelle dying, it didn't seem like she would be the one threatening them so it had to be Alex. But what was it he was threatening them with? Death? Custody? Did Alex have something on April, or concoct something about April that would look bad and she'd lose custody of Joey?

That seemed like the most likely scenario, causing her to lose custody of Joey. April wouldn't care about the money, she'd care if Joey was harmed or if she was taken away from her. That would be the most horrible thing for April.

But why wouldn't she share something that terrible with her mother? Was she trying to protect Aunt Carrie? Or, had she tried to handle it on her own and it led to her death?

That had to be it. April was trying to figure a way out of whatever it was Benjamin was warning her about and instead of finding a solution, someone got to her and quieted her before she had a chance to do anything about it, or tell anyone what was going on.

I called Aunt Carrie and asked her if Detective Myer had gotten back to her yet about what Jimmy had said.

"MJ, Detective Myer did return my call, but she didn't seem to have anything of interest to tell me. It seems that Benjamin had merely gone to talk to April to tell her about Estelle's health and to see if April would allow Joey to spend time with them."

That had to be a lie. I told Aunt Carrie I was on my way home and would see her soon. I then stopped at the side of the road and found the number for Detective Myer and gave her a call.

When Detective Myer answered I said, "I just found out more information about what happened between April and Benjamin. Do you want to hear it?"

All I heard was a deep sigh on the other end. I knew she was exasperated by my attempt at being a detective and finding April's murder, but I didn't care.

I went on to tell her what Jimmy said to me earlier.

"Okay, MJ, thanks for giving us this information. Could you write down exactly what Jimmy said and text it to me? We can then decide if we need to return and interview Benjamin again."

The way she said it, I was pretty sure they were not going to be going to interview Benjamin again. I was pretty sure she felt I was being a pain in the ass and didn't know when to leave it alone and allow her and her team to do their job.

Nonetheless, I texted her the information and hoped that she'd at least have another go with Benjamin. Why would he withhold information if it had to do with harm to Joey or April?

I wanted to scream. They weren't taking me seriously. In my gut, I knew there was something way off about the Sparks. I couldn't say what it was exactly, but I knew something was wrong.

I really wasn't sure what to do. Aunt Carrie wanted me to quit nosing around and to leave the Sparks alone. She thought I'd cause trouble and she'd never see Joey again. She was scared. I didn't blame her. I was scared too. I did not trust any of the Sparks at this point.

So what if Estelle had cancer and was dying. She had the means to get whatever she wanted if she paid enough. I wasn't stupid. Money talked. She had billions to help talk for her.

But what about Joey? She was the last heir to the Spark fortune. Why would she need to be protected unless being alive would jeopardize someone else inheriting those billions.

Who stood to lose?

There was only one answer. Benjamin or Alex, but only if Alex was still alive.

Maybe Estelle came to her senses and forgave Alex for whatever it was he did to cause her to disinherit him. Maybe Estelle decided that the money had to stay within the family, and that would be Alex and Joey.

If this were so, then Benjamin was the only one who would lose. Except, based on Jimmy's remarks, it seemed like he was warning April and trying to protect her and Joey, not threaten them.

I needed help with all of this. Hopefully, Detectives Myer and Dunham would be going back to talk to Benjamin again soon, but I didn't have high hopes that they took seriously what I had to tell them. To them, I was just meddling in a murder investigation and was an amateur who didn't know what I was talking about.

But Jesse wouldn't brush me off like that. I needed to call him. Or was I just trying to find another reason to see him? I wasn't sure at that point.

One thing I knew was that I had to go and talk to Estelle and Benjamin myself. And, I had to see for myself that Joey hadn't been harmed.

I decided that it was time for me to go pay a visit. Except I had no idea where Estelle and Benjamin lived.

Jesse would be able to find their address. I was sure of it. Things were available to him that weren't available to someone like me. I made the call.

I wasn't sure he'd answer my call after how we left it the night before, but he answered on the second ring.

"Hey, MJ." He sounded tired and wary and I couldn't blame him with me pulling him in and then pushing him back out.

"Jesse," I started, but wasn't quite sure how to continue. He didn't help make it easy for me.

"I need a favor."

"Of course you do."

"Jesse, I have more information since I saw you last night and I really need to go talk to the Sparks. Can you get me their address?"

There was more silence on his end and after waiting a while, I said, "Hello, are you still there?"

"I'm here, MJ. I just don't know what to say to you."

"Do you have the ability to find me the Sparks address?"

"I may have."

"Would you be able to get it for me?"

"What is it exactly you need to talk to them about, MJ?"

"I need to find out the truth."

"The truth. About what?"

"About Estelle's will, about where Alex is, about everything."

"Why on earth do you think they'll tell you the truth?"

"Maybe they won't, but I'll be able to get more information by talking to them in person. I'm sure of it. Plus, I really need to see if Joey is okay. I can't let anything bad happen to her."

"MJ, this is a really bad idea. I don't know if I could get you their address, even if I wanted to."

Rage filled my heart and I said in a very tight voice, "Don't bother, Jesse. I'll find it another way."

I wished I had had an old type of phone, so I could have banged the receiver down in his ear. But ending the call abruptly just as he started to say something, was almost as satisfying.

I called Franny and asked her if she could get Peter to get the Sparks address. She told me it wouldn't be a problem and that she'd get back to me, although she hesitated and wondered why I needed it.

"You really don't need that information, Franny. Just, thank you."

No Witnesses

I waited for maybe twenty minutes until Franny called me back with the address.

"MJ, you aren't going over there to cause trouble, are you?"

"The less you know, the better it will be for you," I told her. Because, truthfully, I was kind of playing all of this by ear and pure gut intuition.

Chapter 40

Armed with the address and nothing else but my fury, I drove for what seemed like hours to an address in Malibu. When I got there, it looked like an estate right on the cliff overlooking the Pacific Ocean. Of course there was a gate that had to be navigated before I'd be able to gain access to the house—and to Joey.

It was an impressive place and I felt intimidated. My thoughts began to play tricks on me: I wondered if maybe there was nothing to be gained by talking to the Sparks. I thought that I may have overreacted.

But just visualizing little Joey and her baby talk that didn't include r's made me angry all over again that she had been taken from the one person she felt safe with. I owed Aunt Carrie what I was about to do. They couldn't possibly hold Aunt Carrie accountable for what I did. She never asked me to do anything and in fact told me to keep out of it.

I almost turned around and drove back to Venice, but then, without even thinking it through, I turned into the drive, rolled my window down, and punched the speaker button. I was pretty sure they could see who I was, because a place like theirs would have a camera correctly placed.

I looked around to see if I could tell where it was, but could not. It was well-hidden, for sure.

A deep male voice asked who I was and for what purpose I was there.

I told the voice my name and that I had come to see Estelle and Benjamin.

The voice once again asked what was the purpose of my visit.

I told the voice that it was none of his business but to tell the Sparks I was there and that it was urgent that I talk to them.

"Just one moment," said the voice.

I rolled my eyes at all the pretense and tried to wait calmly.

It was a surprise when I heard the gate start to slowly open.

When there was enough room for my car, I began the long winding drive up to the impressive, Tudor style house.

Tudor was not my favorite style, it always feels heavy and dark to me, but I wasn't surprised since I felt Estelle herself to be heavy and dark.

I was greeted by a woman in her early forties who appeared dressed in dark, simple, traditional clothing. She didn't smile as she told me to follow her.

I assumed she was a personal assistant to Estelle. She showed me into a room where Estelle was sitting at a small table that held a silver coffee set with two cups and saucers. It looked like she was expecting me, but assumed that people of their means had a highly efficient staff who anticipated their every little whim.

"Hello, Estelle," I said.

"Ms. Lange, forgive me, but why are you here? Didn't we already go over everything last time we met?"

Her voice was dripping with pomposity as she poured coffee into each delicate cup. She asked if I took cream or sugar and then handed me the cup of black coffee after I gestured that I wanted neither.

I have to admit, I felt very intimidated. I am from a humble family who had very little in terms of finances, so I wasn't used to being in a place that had such abundance, although it felt dark and sad to me.

"I think you know why I'm here, Estelle. I need to see Joey to make sure she's okay. There's something going on here, I can sense it. I know it has something to do with all of your money. I just don't want Joey to get caught up in all of your games. She's an innocent child and shouldn't have to suffer because of what is going on with you and your money."

She arched a thin eyebrow as she looked down her aristocratic nose at me and said, "So you think you have it all figured out, do you?"

"You're dying. Something's changed because of it. I think you changed your will. I think you're leaving all your money to Joey so your son and husband won't get any of it. You've had a change of heart regarding your granddaughter. You want to make it up to her, so you plucked her out of her nana's lap in order to indulge your needs. Only you don't really care about Joey so much as you care about using your money to inflict pain onto others."

She threw her head back and laughed, or I thought it was a laugh.

I remained quiet.

"Well, you certainly were resourceful enough to find out about my cancer. I wonder how you managed that."

"Does it really matter, Estelle?"

Her shoulders seemed to slump at that and she took a sip of her coffee. I did the same as I mirrored her. I had to admit that the coffee was delicious.

"Okay, so you know I'm dying. So what? Why are you here? What business is it of yours anyway? What is it you want? Is it money?"

It was my turn to laugh. "I don't need nor do I care about your frickin' money. What I want is to see Joey. I need to see that she's all right."

She furrowed her brow and said, "Why wouldn't she be? She has a household of maids and nannies all devoted to her care and her whims. She does not want for anything."

"Except for love from her nana."

"She'll get over that. She just needs time to get used to all of this."

"Can I see her?"

I thought she was going to deny me as she contemplated my request.

"Oh, all right." She clapped her hands and the woman who had greeted me earlier seemed to appear out of nowhere.

"Penny, bring Joey here. Tell her that Ms. Lange is here to see her."

"Tell her it's MJ. She won't know who Ms. Lange is," I quickly clarified for Penny.

We sat in silence as Penny went to find Joey. I held my breath as we waited while staring at each other. Neither one of us spoke.

After an intense ten minutes or so, I could hear the little girl's voice asking questions of Penny, who remained steadfastly silent.

When Joey came into the room, she had on a frilly dress that I had never seen before and it did not become her. Her hair was parted in the middle and two severely tight braids fell down her back. I hardly recognized her. Where were her blond curls?

When she saw me, her face lit up in a happy smile and she ran to me and pitched herself into my lap, giggling and crying at the same time.

I grabbed and hugged her close, tears in my own eyes. I forgot that Estelle and Penny were there, watching. I didn't care. I held on to Joey and she nestled her little face into my neck with her arms around me, holding on tight.

After we held each other and she loosened her grip, we looked at each other and Joey said, "You came to get me. I knew you would."

I looked over at Estelle and caught a look that said it all.

Chapter 41

Estelle's eyes were boring into mine with such hatred, I had to gasp. I had never seen that kind of loathing toward me before. Was she jealous of me that Joey seemed to willingly come to me for comfort?

Well, it was her own fault. Maybe if she wasn't such a cold bitch, Joey would warm to her.

As I cuddled Joey, I looked at Estelle and returned her stare with my own form of fire. I didn't hate her, but I also sat up straighter and was determined not to let her intimidate me. She was totally unfit to be any kind of a grandparent.

Just then, Benjamin came into the room. He stopped short. I guess he hadn't gotten the memo that I was in the house. There was a heavy silence as he stood and gaped at me holding Joey.

I hadn't even noticed that Estelle's assistant had left the room until she came scurrying back with a look of fear. She leaned down and whispered something into Estelle's ear and I wondered what was causing the concern in her eyes.

It soon became clear that Detectives Myer and Dunham were waiting with a warrant and Penny was trying to warn Estelle before they came barging into the room.

My only thought was to thank God someone sane was here with me. I was glad they had finally come to talk to Benjamin again now that they knew what Jimmy had said to me. At the same time, I was a little disappointed. When I had seen Benjamin come into the room, I had thought it was a great opportunity for me to quiz him on what he had said to April that made her cry. Now I wasn't sure I'd get that chance.

I was as surprised as Benjamin when Detective Myer advanced toward him and asked, "Benjamin Spark?" When he answered in the affirmative she said, "Benjamin Spark, you are under arrest for the murder of April Petersen."

I held Joey close to me and gasped. I had my suspicions about Benjamin, but had come to the conclusion that he had gone to warn April; not to kill her. But now it started to make sense to me that it was Benjamin, since Alex wasn't his biological son. He may have killed both April and Alex and then hid Alex's body somewhere no one will ever find. He may have been plotted these murders after finding out that Estelle cut him out of her will.

After being read his Miranda rights, Benjamin kept remarkably quiet, his mouth clamped together in a tight line as he looked with hatred at Estelle.

Estelle, on the other hand, didn't seem the least bit upset or sorry that this was happening. I kept looking from one to the other, trying to figure out what the hell was going on.

Detective Myer was not forthcoming and refused to answer any of my questions, except to say that they found evidence that indicated Benjamin killed April.

I looked on as they led Benjamin out the door. I had a difficult time actually believing that Benjamin had the guts to kill someone. I thought it had to be a mistake, but with Alex still missing, I guessed it was possible.

Joey started to cry and I tried to sooth her by telling her that we were going to ask Grandma Estelle if we could go visit with Nana. This news stopped the tears and she asked if we could go right away. She said that she had so much to tell Nana and me. She told me that she did not like living with Estelle.

I couldn't help smiling at her ability to stay in the moment. I asked Estelle if I could take her for an overnight with Aunt Carrie. I needed to get her out of this house that was obviously causing her distress. I also added that Aunt Carrie was working with her lawyer to try to get shared custody for Joey.

Estelle remained quiet as she motioned to her assistant Penny and told her something in a low voice. She had her hand covering her mouth so I was unable to read her lips and the low tones were outside of my hearing range.

I repeated my request to which she answered, "We'll see. Let's just wait here a moment."

I was feeling anxious. My intuition started to kick in as I felt more and more that something was up and it probably wasn't going to be something good.

It seemed like we sat there forever, with Joey babbling away about wanting to change her clothes and take the braids out of her hair. She said the braids hurt her head.

To my surprise, the door opened and Alex walked into the room, "You."

"Surprised to see me, MJ?"

Joey turned her head into my chest and I could hear her whimper. She really did not like her father, and neither did I.

I thought about making a run for it with Joey, but knew that wouldn't work with all the staff around, plus I'd be too slow carrying a child. I wasn't sure what was in play. I didn't get the feeling that I was in danger, but these people played to win. And they wanted Joey.

The only tool I had at my disposal was my mouth. I knew, as a psychologist that people were trained to answer questions. So I started asking questions fast and furiously.

"You didn't seem very surprised or upset that Benjamin was arrested, Estelle. Why is that? Did you know he killed April, or did you tell him to kill her?"

There was only silence, but I saw Alex smirk at me, like he knew it all.

"How long do you have to live before you die from your cancer? It must gall you that you won't be alive to see whatever it is you have going here come into fruition, right?" I was guessing at this point. So many things didn't make sense to me and I was puzzled and needed some answers. Like, where did Alex come from? Was he hiding out at Estelle's all along? And if so, Estelle had to know about it and kept quiet this whole time. But my primary goal was to get Joey out of that awful house and to safety.

At the mention of her cancer, Estelle scoffed and dismissed it with her hand.

"My mother doesn't have cancer," Alex said.

This time, I definitely looked puzzled, "But I thought. . ."

"Yes, yes, you and your darling little cop friend think you're so smart," Estelle sniffed.

"You don't have cancer? Then how. . . . why . . ?"

"My mother is very clever, and she has a lot of friends who will do anything for her for a price. She planted the cancer. . . . "

"Alex, shut up! You never could keep your mouth shut. You are a blooming idiot. Penny, come take Joey."

I held tightly to Joey. No one was going to take her from me.

"Oh, MJ, come, come. Don't be difficult and so suspicious. I'm merely asking her to take Joey to get her ready to go with you for an overnight with her precious nana."

I wasn't sure what to do. I was outnumbered and she sounded reasonable. No one was threatening me or Joey. But I didn't trust Estelle.

Penny stood calmly waiting to take Joey while Estelle sat in her chair and seemed at ease. Alex took a package of cigarettes from his suit coat, but before he could light one, Estelle told him he couldn't smoke in the house. Things seemed somewhat ordinary and nothing I could see stood out as a danger, so I said, "Okay, Joey, go with Penny. I'll be right here to take you to see Nana. I won't leave without you. I promise."

I stood and watched her leave, her little head turned to look back at me with a frown on her face.

At that moment, I knew I had made a fatal mistake.

Chapter 42

I was staring at a gun aimed directly at my stomach. Estelle stood erect with a nasty grin on her face. I froze for a moment, not comprehending what I was seeing. Estelle with a gun, pointed at me. There was an unreality to the whole situation and my first thought was how I'd be able to protect Joey when she came back.

Suddenly, I had the horrific realization that Joey was most likely not coming back and Estelle had her removed in order to kill me without Joey being present.

This was not the first time I had a gun aimed at me, nor was it the first time my life was in danger. I had survived the prior two times, but this felt different. This time I could not see any way out. I put my hands up and felt myself dissociating from my body. I felt like I was looking down at myself and felt frozen in time.

I closed my eyes waiting to hear the gun go off, when, instead, I heard my phone ring in my pant pocket. When I automatically started to reach for it, Estelle said, "Don't answer that."

"Okay, okay. I won't. I'm just going to put my hand in my pocket to retrieve it and shut it off."

"No, no you don't. Take it out slowly and hand it to Alex."

I nodded and slowly took the phone out, glancing to see that it was Jesse. As I put both of my hands up over my head, I was able to push the answer button and said out-loud, hoping Jesse could hear me. "Estelle, you don't want to do this. Put your gun away."

Alex had been pacing back and forth, his adrenaline pumping. "Shut up. Shut up. Hand me your phone."

When I hesitated he barked out loudly, "NOW!"

"Okay, okay, I'll give you my phone, Alex." I hoped that Jesse heard me say Alex, so whatever happened to me, they'd know that Alex was involved.

That was all I could do, and watched as he threw it on the floor and stomped on it, shattering it to bits and pieces. I prayed Jesse had heard me and would be able to get help to me as quickly as possible.

I had to find a way to stall them. The only thing that kept me from fainting from fear was that little girl waiting patiently in her room happily anticipating her reunion with her grandmother and me. Tears came to my eyes as I considered that I had failed her and her nana.

My voice shaky, I asked, "So, Estelle, what's the plan here? The police were just here, they saw me with you. Joey's good at telling what she's seen and heard. You're just going to shoot me right here in your house? It won't mesh with Penny and Joey's stories."

I knew there was no hope that Penny would tell the truth, and Joey was only four years old. Of course, I was bluffing and at the same time trying to stall.

"MJ, you have no idea the lengths I will go to protect what's mine. I'm not going to just shoot you here. No, no, the story is that Alex appeared out of nowhere with a gun. He was quite distraught, waving it all over the place, threatening you and me. You see, he had disappeared after strangling April in one of his rages until today when he showed up with the gun. Fortunately, I was able to wrestle the gun from him, but, unfortunately, not before he shoots you."

Alex stopped short and looked at his mother wild-eyed and said, "What? It was your idea to strangle April. It was you who made the plan to kill her. You promised me that if I killed her, you'd reinstate me in your will."

"Oh, Alex, you were never a very clever boy. But I guess it won't hurt now that you are blabbing away, telling her all our secrets. She won't be around to tell anyway. And neither will you."

As she spoke to Alex, she pointed the gun at him and my mind started racing, trying to figure out how to get the gun away from her. I decided that the best thing to do was to keep them talking so I asked, "Why kill April? What had she done to deserve that? What possible reason could you have had to kill her?"

Ignoring my questions, Estelle went on, enjoying her control over us, delighting in her wicked plan. "Actually, Alex, you confessed to the both of us as you were waving your gun around. Then, you pointed it at me and MJ lunged at you, but she was too slow and you shot her. You were so shocked when you actually pulled the trigger that you paused for a moment just as the momentum of MJ lunging at you caused her to fall over onto you. I was able to grab your gun and fire it into your heart."

Alex and I both stared at Estelle. It was such a ridiculous story. How was she going to make it look like I lunged at Alex? No one would ever believe it. Especially if Jesse was able to hear my message.

"Estelle, stop and think about this. You'll never get away with it. So far, you've not killed anyone. I'm sure with all of your money you can find a lawyer that can make any part of your participation in April's murder go away. But if you kill Alex and me and come up with that story, you'll most likely go away for a very long time."

I couldn't tell if she was listening to me, or to whatever was inside her sick head. Her gun was pointed at Alex so I contemplated making a rush toward her, but I had a gut feeling that I'd never make it. I looked around desperately for something to throw at her or distract her and I wondered where the hell Penny was.

And where were the cops? Surely Jesse heard my plea and called it in. Since I didn't hear any sirens, I knew I was on my own.

I guessed I couldn't count on Alex helping because he wouldn't want to keep me alive, especially since I was a witness to his confession.

Before any of us could make a move, we heard a little faint knock and the three of us as a unit turned to look at where the knock was coming from. It was the door Penny had taken Joey through not fifteen minutes ago.

I knew that little knock. It was Joey. I was sure of it.

In an instant, as Estelle was distracted by the sound of the knock, I ran toward her and did a baseball slide into Estelle's feet. Her feet flipped up and over and she went down onto her back with a cry of pain, letting the gun fly out of her hand.

I didn't wait to see how she was, but got up and ran to the door where I heard the knock. It was Joey, so tiny and scared. I scooped her up and started toward the door to freedom.

But as I reached for the doorknob, I heard the sound of a gun discharging and stopped cold.

I turned around to see that Alex was the one with the gun now and Estelle was lying on the floor with blood spilling out of her chest. With Joey still in my arms, I looked at Alex, waiting to see what he was going to do next.

Chapter 43

I reached out my free hand in supplication, "Alex, you don't want to do this. You don't want to become like your mother. If you shoot now, you might hurt your daughter. Let me put her down."

He stood there aiming his gun at us. We could hear sirens in the distance. Finally. They were getting closer and closer. I could see that Alex didn't know what to do. We were at a standstill and all I could think to do was to keep talking. To ask questions. So that was what I did.

"Alex, you didn't want to kill April. You aren't a murderer."

"She," he said, pointing at Estelle, "was the one who made the plan to kill April. She had it all planned. She lured April out of the house and down the back steps, had me hide behind her and sneak up on her with my belt and strangle her."

He put his hands up to his face and cried out, "Oh god, it was awful. I can still feel the life leaking out of her. It seemed to take forever, but Estelle wouldn't let me stop. She just kept telling me to pull the belt tighter, tighter, tighter!"

My stomach clenched and I almost threw up realizing just how evil this woman was. Enticing her son to kill his child's mother with the promise of money. And then the plan to kill him, making up a story of self defense, blaming him for killing me too; getting away, herself, scot-free.

But it hadn't turned out in her favor. I heard the sirens get closer and closer. As Alex was reliving April's death, I quickly lunged for the door and with Joey clutched to my breast, ran until we reached the outside door to freedom.

Once we were out in the clean fresh ocean air, I was shaking so badly that I thought I was going to drop Joey. I sat on the steps of that ugly Tudor, Joey on my lap, and watched as the police came.

There were about four police cars, followed by an ambulance. They approached me with caution, shouting at me to let the child go. I tried, but Joey clung to my neck and wouldn't allow it, so I put my hands up so they could see that I didn't have a weapon.

When they got to me, they pried Joey away from me and I felt helpless as she screamed and kicked at the officers. I tried to tell her to go with them, that I would be with her in a minute, but she was too upset to hear me.

Two of the officers handcuffed me and several of the other officers raced into the house, weapons drawn. I tried to warn them that Alex had a gun, but no one was listening to me. I saw several more officers hiding behind their police car doors, weapons drawn and pointed at the house.

It was a nightmare and I felt like I was in some kind of movie. It was all surreal.

After I was placed in the back of one of the police cars, I saw the police that entered the Tudor come out, along with Penny and several other people who I presumed were staff.

Alex wasn't amongst them.

I hadn't heard any gunshots, so he hadn't had a shootout with them. *Where was he?*

I sat in the back of the police car, shaking from shock and listened to Joey screaming for me. I couldn't do anything and felt helpless. All I wanted to do was go and comfort her. I still hadn't understood the full extent of what I had just witnessed.

They had arrested Benjamin for murdering April because they had some kind of evidence proving he did it. But then Alex and Estelle had just admitted that they murdered her. And for what reason, they never said. They must have planted the evidence that pointed to Benjamin.

Estelle did not have cancer, and Alex had not disappeared, but was being sheltered by his estranged mother who then was going to kill him and me and frame Alex for killing me. She must have had this entire thing planned out from the very beginning.

If Joey hadn't come when she did and knocked on the door enough to distract Estelle, I believe Estelle would have gotten away with it. She was rich and powerful and whatever she told the police, they would have believed. Except Jesse must have heard me because the cavalry came. He would have been able to counter her statement. But she was extremely powerful and most likely would have told the original story she had planned and gotten away with it.

As I sat in the car, I wondered where Jesse was. I still didn't know if Estelle was alive or dead, and had no idea why I wasn't seeing Alex anywhere.

Trying to shut Joey's screams out, I leaned my head back on the seat and closed my eyes, my handcuffs biting into my wrists, but I hardly felt them. I was just relieved that Joey was alive; and me too.

I must have drifted off from sheer fatigue when I heard the door open, "MJ, it's me."

My eyes opened and I saw Jesse bending in to get into the back seat. I burst into tears and he engulfed me in his powerful arms as he shouted out to one of the officers to take the damn handcuffs off me.

Joey had stopped screaming and there was a quiet hush that surrounded me as the cuffs were being taken off.

"Where's Joey? My god, where is Joey?"

"Shhhh, shhhh, MJ, she's okay. Let me take you to see her."

Policemen were scattered around the pristine yard. I could see Penny sitting on one of the benches talking to one of the policewomen. We walked to where the ambulance was and that is where I found my Joey.

She was sitting on the opened back part of the ambulance, a blanket wrapped snugly around her. She was eating a chocolate bar while talking a mile a minute to one of the EMTs.

When she saw me, her face lit up, she threw her blanket off, jumped from where she was sitting and ran to me. I knelt and scooped her up.

"Jesse, you have to call Aunt Carrie and tell her Joey is okay." Then I turned to Joey and asked if she'd like to go see her nana.

Chapter 44

It wasn't over. There was a lot to sort out. I was made to stay and answer questions. There was a bit of chaos surrounding me.

After learning that Estelle had been shot and killed, they were questioning me as to what had happened. There was no gun to be found, and I think they were suspicious of me, especially since Alex was not around.

Of course there were new detectives on the case, since it was Malibu and not Venice where Detectives Myer and Dunham were in charge.

Jesse gave his statement as to what he had heard on my phone, but it didn't compute with what they found in the house. It was confusing and it all needed to be sorted out.

I wondered if Penny would remain loyal to Estelle, or if she would tell the truth. I was still in shock, so I wasn't sure if she had actually seen Alex, or if Alex came into the room after she had left with Joey. It was all so confusing. I just wanted to go home and crawl into bed and sleep for a month.

Apparently, they were able to sort things out enough in order to release me and I was able to take Joey with me in my car to go home. I had called Aunt Carrie and she was waiting for us. I'm sure she'd have a lot of questions that I didn't have the answers to. The main thing was that Joey was coming back home with us. That was all that mattered.

After assessing me to make sure I was capable of driving, Jesse followed us back home to make sure we arrived safely. Since Joey had fallen asleep in the car, Jesse carried her into Aunt Carrie's house and put her gently on her bed as we watched Aunt Carrie remove her shoes, cover her with a blanket and then kiss her gently on her forehead.

We gathered in the kitchen and Jesse told us as much as he knew. Aunt Carrie made us coffee and set out a plate of chocolate chip cookies for us, keeping us going with caffeine and sugar.

I let the hot coffee warm my chilled and shaken body. It was a wonder that I was able to even drive home, but when I was there at Aunt Carrie's table with Jesse sitting across from me and Aunt Carrie sitting next to me, I finally was able to fall apart.

Aunt Carrie got up and brought a warm blanket to throw over my shoulders. Jesse came over and put his arms around me and let me sob into his broad shoulders.

It had been a lot. I was in a life and death situation after which I was handcuffed and accused and almost arrested for the murder of Estelle. But the biggest upset for me was hearing Joey screaming for me and I was not able to do anything about it.

No Witnesses

I blubbered all of this to them as they soothed and pampered me, petting my hair and patting my hands, encouraging me to drink my coffee. I heard them arguing about whether or not to put a shot of bourbon into it.

Aunt Carrie won out and I wasn't sure if I was grateful to her or not. I really wanted that shot of bourbon. Surely the ordeal I had just gone through must have been worth some kind of Hail Mary in terms of my sobriety.

They finally got me to go into Aunt Carrie's room to lie on the bed, covered me up and sat beside me until I drifted off into a troubled sleep.

I woke and noticed hours must have passed because it looked like twilight out the window. I could hear voices in the kitchen and realized that there were more people than Jesse and Aunt Carrie. I couldn't hear what they were saying, but could hear the uneasiness in their tone.

The blanket that had warmed me felt heavy and hot, so I pulled it off and with an unsteady gait, shuffled into the kitchen to see what was happening.

Detectives Myer and Dunham were there, as was Franny. They were sitting around the table with Jesse and Aunt Carrie. They all looked up at me as I entered the kitchen and stopped talking.

"What's happened?" I asked.

Aunt Carrie hurried toward me and ushered me to an empty chair, saying, "Come and sit down, MJ. How are you feeling?"

After assessing myself and deciding I was okay, they all breathed a sigh of relief.

"MJ, we were really concerned about you and weren't sure if we should have called a doctor or taken you to the emergency room. You were very close to being in physical shock."

Aunt Carrie then got up and poured a glass of water and demanded that I drink it.

They all watched as I sipped on the water and, feeling rather foolish, I said, "Hey guys, I'm okay. I'm really okay. What's going on?"

They all looked at each other. The look on their faces alerted me to question what was going on. "What?" I asked.

Aunt Carrie looked down at her coffee and shook her head.

"What is it? You have to tell me."

Jessie got up and indicated to Detective Myer that she should speak.

"MJ, Estelle's assistant, Penny White, did confirm that Alex had been there. So your story does check out. However, there is no sign of Alex anywhere. He was able to escape."

"What? That's impossible. He was right there in that room where Estelle was shot. I saw him there. There was only one other door in that room that must have led to where Joey was being kept. There's no way he could have gotten out."

They looked at each other again with that look.

"There's more."

"Just tell me already."

"We found Benjamin dead in his holding cell after we got back from Malibu. Somebody got to him. We know now that he didn't kill April, based on your testimony. We assume that he knew some vital information as to why they killed April, but he's been silenced."

I put my hand to my mouth and said, "So, Estelle and Alex got away with murdering April, and Estelle was able to hire a hit on Benjamin. Without Alex or Benjamin we don't have anyone to tell us why all of this happened. And Estelle's plan would have worked since there would have been no witnesses, right?"

Jesse came back to the table with a scowl and said, "Yup, that's it in a nutshell."

I knew exactly what he was thinking, that if the detectives had questioned Benjamin when we asked them to, about what he had said to April, we'd have the motivation. But it was too late because Benjamin was dead.

It was difficult for me not to shout at them and blame them for their incompetence, so I asked instead, "What happens now?"

"We've got an APB out for Alex, so hopefully we'll apprehend him and get some answers. He can't have gone far."

I sat at the table and stared. "Is Joey or Aunt Carrie in any danger? Am I?"

"We don't think so. We think he's scared and running. The way he was able to disappear after he killed April may be how he's been able to disappear now. We're searching the Tudor now and have warned Penny and staff not to go anywhere. We need to do more intensive interviews with them. Someone knows something."

"Why are you here then and not out there searching and interviewing? You've got to catch him."

"We came in hopes that Joey would be able to shed some light on this. Maybe she saw something or heard something, but she's still fast asleep. It's getting late, so we'll circle around tomorrow."

After we all said good night to the detectives, I sat down again at the kitchen table with Jesse, Franny, and Aunt Carrie. As I sat there, a germ of an idea came to me. The longer we sat in silence, the more the idea appealed to me.

"What are you thinking, MJ?" Franny said. "I know that look."

Chapter 45

The next morning, Aunt Carrie, Joey, and I sat at the kitchen table and ate the sweet rolls Aunt Carrie set out for us. Joey had her orange juice, and Aunt Carrie and I had our coffee.

It almost all seemed normal, like no one was murdered, or shot, or disappeared. I looked over at Joey delicately picking at her sweet roll with her tiny fingers. She didn't seem to be traumatized at all, but we'd have to wait and see how she managed in the coming days and weeks.

I smiled at her and asked, "Hey, Joey, would you like to come over to my place and play with me later on today?"

She smiled and clapped her hands in anticipation of a play date and told us that she really missed us and didn't like that adventure at all.

I hugged Aunt Carrie and Joey good-bye and left to go to my place, showered and then headed out the door to go buy Joey a playhouse with little play human figures.

I had a plan and I hoped that it might work.

Later, after lunch, I arrived at Aunt Carrie's to pick Joey up for our play date. The detectives had come earlier to ask Joey about what she may have heard or seen at Estelle's. She hadn't been able to give them any more details than they already knew. They had told Aunt Carrie that they were still trying to find how Alex was able to escape so easily.

When Joey and I arrived at my apartment, I gave her the play dollhouse and the figures and we set out to play. As if I had just thought of it, I asked, "How about we set up the house like it was the day Benjamin came to talk to your mommy?"

"Okay." And she went about selecting which figure was her mommy and which was Benjamin. She then told me that the little girl and the little boy were Joey and Jimmy.

I felt an excitement run through me when I realized that Joey had been there the day Benjamin made April cry.

"Okay, Joey, this is great. Why don't you play all the parts first, so I know what happened. Then I'll be able to play when we do it again. I could maybe be your mommy and Benjamin, and you could be Joey and Jimmy."

"Okay, MJ."

I then told her that we should make a movie of it and she helped me set up my cellphone positioned to record the scene. I wanted a recording of this, just in case something important was revealed.

I sat quietly so she wouldn't be spooked or distracted. I waited for her to set up where all the characters had been that day when her mommy cried with Benjamin. When she had it set up, I asked her to play act what had happened.

She went through moving her figures around, having her mother let Benjamin in the house reluctantly, then had Jimmy come in and ask if he could borrow some of Joey's art materials for his project and had April tell him where they were. Joey had apparently followed Jimmy into her room to get the materials. Then Joey came out to where April and Benjamin were sitting in the living room across from each other.

This is where I learned the truth.

Joey had the Joey figure stay in the doorway to the living room. Then Joey used her deep, male voice for Benjamin and said, "Apwil, don't be a fool. Estelle can make you wook bad. Let Alex take her. You can have visishun. Estelle can and will make you look bad if you don't coopawate and you'll neva see Joey again."

She then scrunched up her little face and said, "I can't wemembe it all, MJ."

"You're doing just fine, Little One. Is there anything else?"

Joey then had the figure that was Jimmy come out of her bedroom and the dialogue began again, as Joey had her mother cry.

In her deep male voice used for Benjamin, she continued: "You know I'm wight, Apwil. I'm the only one who can pwotect you and Joey. Do the wight thing."

Joey then had Benjamin leave and I stopped the role play.

"Joey, you did good. I have it all on the phone now. We can continue to play later today or tomorrow, but I need to show this movie to someone important now."

Joey looked up at me and said, "Okay."

Chapter 46

The first thing we did was translate Joey's words into words the police could understand, putting the R's in, and putting in words that had been too difficult for Joey to comprehend.

So the dialogue of Benjamin was this: "April, don't be a fool. Estelle can make you look bad. Let Alex take her. You can have visitations. Estelle can and will make you look bad if you don't cooperate and you'll never see Joey again."

After showing the detectives the role-play Joey had done, they were able to get a warrant for Estelle's will and trust and other important documents her lawyer had.

It was all about the money. Enough money to make Estelle willing to lie and kill. She was indeed an evil woman and I, for one, was glad Alex shot her, except I would have loved to see her rot in prison.

As Jesse, Aunt Carrie, Franny and I sat with detectives Myer and Dunham for our final debriefing, it was pretty clear what had happened.

Apparently, Detective Myer told us, Estelle's grandfather wasn't a very nice man either and he had laid down some heavy stipulations before the next generations could inherit his billions. It seemed like he loved playing with people's emotions and minds, using his money to set up the future so he could still manipulate from his grave. *What a piece of work.*

For one, if there were no male heirs, then the female heir would have to carry on the family name, marrying only someone who would agree to take on her surname, which is what Estelle did by having her husbands take on the name of Spark. I guess grandpa Spark's ego couldn't tolerate it if his name didn't continue to carry on.

What got more complicated was that when the next generation heir turned a certain age, half of the Spark money would go to that heir, which would be the first born, unless that heir had died. Then, half the money would immediately go to the first born of the following generation. That would have been Joey if Alex had died. At least I think that's how it was set up. It was all pretty convoluted.

Estelle had disowned Alex when he defied her for something we still don't know about. The stipulation of Estelle's grandfather did not allow for her to disown her son, so Alex was slated to get half of her billions on his next birthday that was coming up. Alex hadn't known anything about it, which is probably why he went along with Estelle's plan.

Estelle had most likely planned this entire scenario from the moment she had disowned Alex. She knew that when Joey inherited all that money, at Joey's age, someone would have to be in charge of the money. She wanted it to be her, so she hatched a scheme to get custody of Joey. In order to get custody, April needed to be out of the picture.

She had originally schemed with Alex, apparently promising and giving him a large cash amount, for him to get full custody of Joey, while manipulating the system to get Joey away from April. She was going to claim that April was an unfit mother who would never be able to get custody of Joey again.

Once Alex had full custody and April was proven unfit, it would have been easy for her to get full custody of Joey. Estelle most likely told Alex that when she disinherited him, he wouldn't be able to get any of the billions. Giving him a large cash payment obviously appealed to him and he went along with it, but what he didn't know is that Estelle had a plan for Alex to disappear forever. Detective Myer wasn't sure if that meant eventually having him killed or having him just disappear. If he was wanted for April's murder, that would ensure that he would not reappear. Estelle would have control of all of the money until Alex was pronounced legally dead.

I wasn't fully understanding. "So why kill April then? Why not move forward with her plan to get custody of Joey, so she would still have control of all the money? That was her plan, right? To have control of all the money? She didn't want Alex getting half."

"Yes, the plan was to smear April and have Alex get full custody of Joey, and then have Alex disappear. But when Benjamin went and told April about the plan, April must have confronted Estelle. We have phone call records that prove the two of them had a twenty minute phone conversation several days after Benjamin had come to warn her. We are speculating Estelle decided that it would work out better if April was dead and Alex wasn't available. She could then get full custody of Joey in order to continue her control over the money. We believe that it was Estelle who offered evidence against Benjamin and then had him killed before we could question him."

Jesse then added, "So, MJ, you going to get Joey gave Estelle the perfect opportunity to get rid of both you and Alex. She most likely hadn't planned that until the opportunity presented itself."

"Oh my god!" I said, "I had no idea I had walked into a hornets' nest. I could have gotten Joey killed."

Aunt Carrie put her hand on mine and said, "But you didn't. You were only doing what you thought was best. How could you have known the extent Estelle would go to keep her billions?"

They still didn't know where Alex was, but assumed that the money Estelle had given him to disappear, and the way she had helped him disappear before, worked again after he shot her. He was out there somewhere with fake documents and probably living in another country by now. We may never know if he's still alive, or where he is.

"Do you think he'll ever come back, and are we in danger from him?" I asked.

"If he does come back, he'll be charged with two accounts of murder, so I doubt he'll try. He's probably in a country with no extradition. I wouldn't worry too much about it."

We all sat in silence, thinking how April's death was such a waste and shouldn't have happened; Benjamin's too.

Joey then came running in with a handful of flowers she had picked from her grandmother's garden. Grinning from ear to ear she said, "These are beautiful, come help me put them in wata. I picked them for you, Nana."

We all laughed and the gloomy spell was broken. Joey was going to be just fine. After all, she was the heiress to a fortune. It was just that with all the rules her great-great grandfather had stipulated, the lawyers would have a time trying to figure out if she actually really got the inheritance after all that happened.

None of us cared. All we cared about was that Joey was with her nana.

I was happy that I got through this without taking a drink and that Joey was living next door, so she would be in my life. Life was starting to feel good again.

I looked over at Jesse and smiled at him. But the smile faded quickly when I saw sadness in his eyes. The case was closed and there was no longer any reason why we would be seeing each other. The joy at having Joey safe and sound living next door to me dwindled as I also realized that I would not be seeing Jesse anymore.

After we all thanked the detectives and ushered them out the door, I turned and saw Jesse hug Aunt Carrie and Joey good-bye. That old familiar feeling came up and I was consumed with loneliness and loss.

He walked over to me and we looked at each other, awash in sadness, until he finally reached out to me and hugged me good-bye. I couldn't stop the tears and clung a moment too long to him as I got control of my emotions.

I then closed the door behind him and turned to face my good friends, trying my best to put on a happy face.

Franny walked up to me and hugged me. I tried to release myself from her hug, knowing what was going to happen if I didn't. She kept holding on tight, rocking me back and forth until my sobs came loud and strong and we stayed that way for a while, until I felt little arms come and hug my legs as Aunt Carrie came and embraced all of us.

My loneliness faded and when I was released from their loving hugs, I wiped my tears with the back of my hand and smiled a genuine smile, one that reached my eyes. Joey said, "MJ's, happy again," as she clapped her hands in glee.

Read More!

Next up for MJ Lange

"No One is Safe"

The fourth in the MJ Lange mystery series will be out soon!

Sign up for my newsletter if you would like to be notified when it is available:

https://cindykludtauthor.com/free-prequel

If you haven't read the first book

"No Caller ID"

You can grab a copy at amazon.com

Https://www.amazon.com/dp/BOB28D1931

Special Request

Thank You For Reading My Book!

I really appreciate all of your feedback and
I love hearing what you have to say.

I need your input to make the next version of this
book and my future books better.

Please take two minutes now to leave a helpful review
on Amazon where you purchased my book.

ACKNOWLEDGMENTS

I wish to acknowledge first and foremost my launch team. You all know who you are. Thank you so very, very much. I appreciate all the time and effort from you.

A big thank you to Ramy Vance, my writing coach and to Myles Holar, my Virtual Assistant. And to Shavonne Clark, developmental editing provided by Edits by Shavonne Clark.

Finally, I wish to acknowledge all the other creative writers out there for inspiration, ideas, and wonderful stories.

AUTHOR BIO

#1 Amazon Best Seller author, Cindy Kludt, uses her experience as a psychotherapist to tell elaborate and chilling tales of her protagonist, psychologist, MJ Lange, who inadvertently gets thrown into dangerous situations involving murder.

Driven by an early desire to understand the complexities of human behavior, this fascination has led Cindy to write suspenseful murder mysteries utilizing her knowledge of the hidden darkness that resides within those who harbor hidden secrets and unresolved conflicts.

Semi-retired and living next door to her 6 year old granddaughter, Cindy lives 10 minutes from Venice Beach, California which inspires her imagination.

www.ingramcontent.com/pod-product-compliance
Lightning Source LLC
Chambersburg PA
CBHW051342040426
42453CB00007B/363